D0560421

MAIN

Marbury v. Madison:

THE COURT'S FOUNDATION

SUPREME COURT MILESTONES

Marbury v. Madison:
THE COURT'S FOUNDATION

CORINNE J. NADEN
AND ROSE BLUE

BENCHMARK BOOKS

MARSHALL CAVENDISH
NEW YORK

Benchmark Books · Marshall Cavendish · 99 White Plains Road
Tarrytown, NY 10591 · www.marshallcavendish.com · Copyright © 2005 Corinne J. Naden and Rose Blue

All Internet sites were available and accurate when sent to press.

Library of Congress Cataloging-in-Publication Data

Naden, Corinne J. · Marbury v. Madison : the Court's foundation / by Corinne J. Naden and Rose
Blue. · p. cm. — (Supreme Court milestones) · Includes bibliographical references and index. ·
ISBN 0-7614-1840-7 · 1. Judicial review—United States—History—Juvenile literature.
2. Separation of powers—United States—History—Juvenile literature. 3. United States. Supreme
Court—History—Juvenile literature. 4. Marbury, William, 1761 or 2-1835—Trials,
litigation, etc.—Juvenile l5.iterature. Madison, James, 1751–1836—Trials, litigation, etc.—
Juvenile literature. I. Title: Marbury versus Madison. II. Blue, Rose. III. Title. IV. Series.
KF4575.Z9N33 2005 · 347.73'12—dc22 · 2004001152

Photo Research by Candlepants Incorporated

Cover Photo: Richard Cummins/Corbis, Sculpture of Chief Justice John Marshall in front of the
Philadelphia Museum of Art. The Supreme Court did not get its own building until 1935.

The photographs in this book are used by permission and through the courtesy of: *Corbis*: Richard
Cummins, 1, 3; Bettmann, 34, 37, 52, 82, 91, 105; Peter Harholdt, 96; 79 (left and right);
Collection of the Supreme Court of the United States: photographer Vic Boswell, 6, 62, 96 (top); *The
Bridgeman Art Library*: Christie's Images, 9; *Art Resource, NY*: 10; National Portrait Gallery,
Smithsonian Institution, 18, 46, 68; The Pierpont Morgan Library, 27; Erich Lessing, 80; The
New York Public Library, 89; *Library of Congress*: (#LC-USZC4-3266) 21, 38, (#LC-USZC4-74) 49,
(#LC-USZ61-1785) 56; *Collection of the Museum for Early Southern Decorative Arts*: 51; *General
Research Division, New York Public Library, Astor, Lenox and Tilden Foundations*: 94, 97; *Franklin D.
Roosevelt Presidential Library*: 100.

Series design by Sonia Chaghatzbanian · Printed in China · 1 3 5 6 4 2

contents

WHO WOULD HAVE THOUGHT THAT AN UNDELIVERED COMMISSION TO APPOINT A JUSTICE OF THE PEACE WOULD CHANGE THE BALANCE OF POWER IN THE UNITED STATES? BECAUSE OF IT, THE NAME OF WILLIAM MARBURY, AN OTHERWISE UNASSUMING JUDGE, IS ETCHED INTO OUR NATION'S HISTORY.

one
SETTING THE STAGE:
THE PLAYERS AND THE TIMES

HISTORY records a GOOD DEaL of what people did but not so much of what they said. A spirited conversation that would have been interesting to hear was the one between Judge William Marbury and newly appointed Secretary of State James Madison back in 1801. Thomas Jefferson had just become the third president of the United States. On the day before Jefferson's inauguration, departing president John Adams had appointed Marbury as a justice of the peace. Marbury's commission was supposed to have been delivered by John Marshall, who served as secretary of state before Madison. Marshall never delivered the commission. Marbury wanted to know where it was.

Madison suggested that Marbury take up the matter with the State Department assistant, clerk Jacob Wagner. What he neglected to add was that once President Jefferson discovered Marbury had not received the commission, he ordered Madison not to deliver it. To Marbury, the matter was suddenly getting very complicated. The judge most likely left Madison's office in an extremely agitated mood.

Thus began perhaps the most important case in the history of the United States Supreme Court. Reaching far beyond the question of Marbury's commission, the Court's decision in this matter established the judiciary as the arbiter and defender of the U.S. Constitution.

Through this power of what is called judicial review, which is not specifically mentioned in the Constitution, the Court asserts its authority to determine the meaning of the Constitution. The Court's decision also stated that the Constitution must always take precedence in any disputes regarding federal or state laws. In this case, the Court for the first time declared a law passed by Congress to be unconstitutional. This momentous decision altered the scope and power of the Supreme Court and changed the history of the United States. With such power, the U.S. court system became an equal partner with the executive and congressional branches in governing the nation. The case is known as *Marbury* v. *Madison* (1803).

THE FRAGILE POLITICAL CLIMATE

The union born of the American Revolution was very young when the stage was set for the *Marbury* case to come before the Supreme Court. The new nation's leaders were still trying to figure out how to govern according to the Constitution they had written in 1787 and put into action in 1788. Before that, the United States of America had been governed under the Articles of Confederation. Even in the aftermath of the victorious independence, the political climate was not as peaceful as one might imagine. Most everyone wanted a strong and law-abiding country. How to get there was a matter of spirited dispute.

The first twelve years had seen two presidents, George Washington for eight years (1789–1797) and John Adams for four (1797–1801). They were both of the same political philosophy, called Federalism, which advocated a strong central government. But political parties were not that important in those early years.

JOHN ADAMS FOLLOWED GEORGE WASHINGTON AS PRESIDENT AND AGREED WITH
HIS POLICIES. THEIR POLITICAL PHILOSOPHY WAS KNOWN AS FEDERALISM.

THE FIRST CABINET IN 1789 CONSISTED OF (FROM LEFT) HENRY KNOX, THOMAS JEFFERSON, EDMUND JENNINGS RANDOLPH, ALEXANDER HAMILTON, AND GEORGE WASHINGTON. THESE WERE THE DAYS BEFORE ANIMOSITIES FLARED.

Washington functioned mainly as a nonpartisan leader through his two terms in office.

Historians agree that the young country could not have picked a more able first leader than George Washington. He was respected by all. He thought that a president should appoint the best people to serve in government regardless of their beliefs. He thought the presidency should be above politics.

Before Adams took office, the fiscal policies of Washington's secretary of the treasury, Alexander Hamilton, had begun to divide the government. Hamilton, a financial wizard and a staunch Federalist, proposed a bold plan that would build a strong union, but it would also weave his own political philosophy into the government. His immediate objectives were to build credit at home and abroad and to strengthen the national government at the expense of the states. Like Washington, Hamilton disliked political parties and felt they made the nation unstable. His idea was to establish a government of superior people who would be above party politics. But the division over his fiscal plan actually hastened the formation of parties. Most of the criticism came from those who defended states' rights since Hamilton's plan would put far more financial power into the federal government. When the disagreement led to the formation of political parties, Hamilton himself became the leader of the Federalist party, which succeeded in electing Adams to the presidency in 1796.

Throughout the 1790s, the policies of the Federalists were more and more criticized, especially in the South. Differences arose over the Jay Treaty with Great Britain, which concerned unpaid war debts and shipping rights. France considered the treaty a violation of its own treaty with the United States and that led to a near war between the two countries. Thomas Jefferson and James Madison began to organize opposition to the Federalists in 1790. Their party became known as the Republican party, later the Jeffersonian-Republicans or the National Republicans—a forerunner of the modern Democratic party.

This testy atmosphere was aggravated by the election of Jefferson in 1800 and the introduction of a new political party in government. Neither party was certain what this change would mean. Republicans read their victory as a demand for change, but even they disagreed among themselves as to the nature of the change.

As for the Federalists, they feared the worst. They were certain that Jefferson was about to destroy the very foundations of the government they had so carefully built over the past twelve years. They had no doubt that the new president would dismantle the military, tear down the courts, and ruin the fledgling economy. Although most Republicans, even Jefferson, were willing to listen to compromise, some such as William Branch Giles of Virginia were loud in their intentions of sweeping change.

THE OUTGOING PRESIDENT

On the evening of March 3, 1801, John Adams was spending his last night in the still unnamed White House. Jefferson would be inaugurated the next day. At that time, the newly elected president and members of Congress did not take office until March 4, four months after election day. Because of slow transportation around the country, it took a long time to get to Washington, D.C.

Adams was never known under the best of circumstances for his cheery disposition, but on the night of March 3, he was almost certainly not in a good mood. First and foremost, he had been defeated in his bid for a second term. Adams had very much wanted another four years as president, considering himself far more qualified for that job than anyone else. In addition, he had real fears for the young government. Federalists had controlled all branches of government for a decade. They feared the changes that Jefferson would bring.

A brilliant lawyer from Braintree (now Quincy), Massachusetts, Adams was just past forty years of age when the American Revolution began. Feeling too old and overweight for military service, he had become a diplomat in France and then in London after the war. When Washington was chosen as the new nation's president, Adams accepted the second spot because he very much wanted to occupy the first. But he hated the job of vice president and found it boring. He spent a good deal of time complaining to his wife, Abigail, that he had nothing of importance to do—a complaint that vice presidents have voiced since, although generally not while still in office. Partly because he was bored and partly because he was a fussbudget, Adams spent his vice presidential years fretting over small details. He concerned himself with matters such as whether he should stand up or sit down when talking to Congress. But, finally, in 1797, at the age of sixty-one, he got the job he really wanted.

For all of his crankiness and fretting, despite his vanity, displays of pompousness, and conceit about his considerable intellect, John Adams was above all a patriot. Like Washington before him and others of that small, remarkable band of early patriots called the Founding Fathers, Adams had but one goal throughout his presidency—the welfare of his beloved country.

An added insult to his defeat after one term, however, was the man who was about to become the third president of the United States: Thomas Jefferson. Adams and Jefferson truly did not like each other. Although that animosity was based mainly on their extremely differing political viewpoints, it was nonetheless real. But the new administration was bringing in a new party and a new political philosophy.

The term "Federalist" was first used to describe the supporters of the new constitution who emphasized the federal character of the country. During the 1790s, the Federalists stood for creating a state bank, maintaining a tariff system, and assuming state debts from the Revolution. In foreign affairs, they tried to stay out of disputes between Great Britain and France. They also favored a strong defense and internal security.

The Jeffersonian Republicans united during the administrations of George Washington because they were against Hamilton's strong fiscal program, such as a strong tariff system that would hamper the states' ability to import and export. They favored states' rights and strict interpretation of the Constitution. That meant they were wary of the federal government taking away too much authority from the states, by setting standards of education or working conditions, for instance. They did not want the federal government to take any more power than was expressly given by the Constitution.

The Jeffersonians used the term "republican" to emphasize the deep antimonarchical feelings of the group, who were greatly influenced by the French revolution.

THE CLOSEST OF FRIENDS

When John Adams left the capital in 1801, he and the new president, Thomas Jefferson, were bitter enemies. Ironically, they would later become the closest of friends. The years apparently mellowed Adams somewhat, so that in 1812, he sent a letter to Monticello, where Jefferson had retired three years earlier. Monticello, near Charlottesville, Virginia, was Jefferson's home, designed and constructed by him in 1775 and added to between 1796 and 1809.

From that first letter followed a long and increasingly close correspondence. The two patriots wrote at length of their memories and their concerns for the new nation.

In 1826 ninety-year-old Adams lay dying. Reportedly, his last words were "Jefferson still lives." But Adams was wrong, for Jefferson had died a few hours earlier at Monticello. Stranger than fiction, the second and third presidents of the United States died on the same day and on the country's birthday, July 4, 1826. It was just fifty years after the signing of the Declaration of Independence.

THE TWELFTH amenDment

The Twelfth Amendment to the U.S. Constitution made some important changes to the way Americans elect their presidents. It eliminated the problem that had occurred when Jefferson was Adams's vice president, despite their entirely different political viewpoints. It said that electors had to vote separately and specifically for the offices of president and vice president. It also stated that candidates for the offices of president and vice president could not come from the same state. The amendment declared that a candidate had to win a majority of the electoral votes in order to be elected. If no candidate had a majority, the House of Representatives would choose a president from among the three candidates with the most electoral votes. If no vice president got a majority, the Senate would choose the winner.

Since the amendment was adopted, only one president has been chosen by the House of Representatives and only one vice president by the Senate. John Quincy Adams, son of John Adams, ran for the presidency in 1824 along with three others, but no one received a majority of the popular vote. Adams was elected by the House in a vote of 13 to 7 over Andrew Jackson. In 1836, Richard M. Johnson ran as vice president on the Democratic ticket headed by Martin Van Buren. Although Van Buren won, no vice presidential candidate had a majority. The choice was left to the Senate, which chose Johnson.

They distrusted so much central power and believed the aristocratic habits of the Federalists leaned a little too much toward royalty.

Adams and the Federalists were certain that Jefferson would "sap the fundamental principles of government." Adams saw the incoming president as a radical who might bring down what he and Washington had so earnestly tried to build. He feared that in the name of individual liberties and states' rights, Jefferson would undermine the strong central government that had been carefully established over the past twelve years.

Strangely enough considering their opposing philosophies, Jefferson had been Adams's vice president. In those early years, the voting ballot did not actually name who was running for what office, president or vice president. The person with the highest number of electoral votes became president, the next highest was vice president. When Adams first ran for president, he received 71 electoral votes to 68 for Jefferson.

Adams lost his second bid for the presidency largely because of his continuing feud with Alexander Hamilton, who was greatly incensed because Adams sometimes voted against the Federalists. Also, Adams had to spend a good deal of time trying to avoid being drawn into endless fighting between Great Britain and France. As the election of 1800 neared, the Federalists were split over actions that Adams had taken to avoid war with France. The anti-French Federalists had wanted war. The Republicans, who were pro-French, declared that Adams was promoting a panic when he urged the Congress to pass bills to prepare the country for military conflict.

Adams and Hamilton had long been political enemies.

THOUGH NEVER ELECTED TO OFFICE, FEDERALIST ALEXANDER HAMILTON PLAYED AN ENORMOUSLY INFLUENTIAL ROLE IN DEFINING OUR COUNTRY'S GOVERNMENT AND ECONOMY.

Before the election, Hamilton wrote an open letter to party leaders about the conduct and character of the president, declaring Adams unfit for public office. That effectively ruined Adams's chances for reelection. The second president was defeated by Jefferson and his running mate Aaron Burr, who each won 73 electoral votes. Adams got 65.

Still operating under a system that did not distinguish between candidates for president and vice president, the election had resulted in a loss for the Federalists but a tie between the two Democratic-Republicans. Jefferson and Aaron Burr each won 73 electoral votes. It was then up to the House of Representatives to choose between them. The House voted thirty-five times by state and still could not break the tie. Finally, on vote number thirty-six, with the influence of hated political enemy Alexander Hamilton, Jefferson won. Hamilton simply distrusted Burr—who would kill him in a duel in 1804—more than he disliked Jefferson.

Adams was so disgruntled about Jefferson's victory that he decided to leave town the next day, deliberately not attending the inauguration of the third president. But now as he sat in his office for the last time in the chilly, damp, and still unfinished White House, he had one last job to do. He was signing commissions for new judgeships. Adams was determined that no matter what changes Jefferson imposed, at least the new president would find die-hard Federalists in various judiciary positions to block his radical policies.

Both Washington and Adams had appointed only Federalist judges to the bench during their terms, and those appointments were for life with "good behavior." After he lost the election of 1800 to a member of the opposition, Adams in the last months of his administration had asked the Federalist-controlled Congress to enlarge the court system by increasing the number of federal judgeships. One way to keep Jefferson from appointing Democratic-Republican judges, especially to the Supreme Court, was to make sure all the positions were already filled.

CREATING THE LEGAL SYSTEM

As Adams expected, Congress responded to his request with the Judiciary Act of 1801, which followed the act of 1789. The Judiciary Act of 1789 has been called one of the most important works of Congress because it created the American legal system. It called for a pyramid structure of the federal courts. At the bottom of the pyramid are the district courts. In the middle are the circuit courts. And at the top of the pyramid is the Supreme Court.

The U.S. *district courts* are entry-level courts, meaning they hear cases concerning criminal and civil matters. The Judiciary Act created thirteen district courts for the thirteen states; today there are ninety-four district courts in the system, with at least one in every state. There are several districts in the largest and most heavily populated states.

On the middle level of the legal pyramid are the *circuit courts*, today known as the U.S. Court of Appeals. To appeal means to have a higher court review a proceeding of a lower court. The party making the appeal is the appellant and argues against errors said to be committed by the lower court. These courts have jurisdiction over specified geographical areas and review matters from the district courts in their region. Circuit, or appeals, courts have their own judges who, since 1891, are appointed for life.

CREATED BY THE JUDICIARY ACT OF 1801, CIRCUIT JUDGES LITERALLY RODE TO THE AREAS WHERE THEY HAD JURISDICTION SINCE NO ACTUAL COURTS IN WHICH TO HEAR CASES YET EXISTED.

on the road again

John Marshall spent many long days as a judge "riding the circuit." So did many judges in the early days. Abraham Lincoln rode the circuit as a lawyer. In any case, it meant long hours of bouncing over dirt roads, sometimes with ruts deep enough to topple a carriage. Marshall logged hundreds of hours traveling hundreds of miles each year to bring the U.S. legal system to the people. Just like the post office, the judges were supposed to render justice through rain, snow, and sleet.

Most of the judges hated riding the circuit, whether by stagecoach or horseback. President George Washington appointed an associate justice, Thomas Johnson, to the Supreme Court. But Johnson accepted only on the condition that he be excused from riding circuit.

An amusing, often-told story concerns Marshall on a circuit-riding trip from Richmond, Virginia, to Raleigh, North Carolina, where he was to hold court. On this journey, Marshall was traveling in a stick gig, a wooden chair sitting on two wheels, attached to two shafts, and pulled by a horse. Many of the justices used stick gigs as transportation. Marshall liked this way of traveling because he could often nap while sitting in the chair and bouncing along. But this time, as he was napping, the stick gig ran over a tree branch and tilted. Marshall found himself in an odd position, unable to move right or left.

Marshall sat there for some time trying to figure a way out of his predicament. Along came an elderly black man to his rescue. The man told him to stop trying to move right or left and just back up the horse. Thus rescued, Marshall went on his way. According to the tale, his elderly rescuer is supposed to have said of the chief justice of the United States, "he's a nice old gentleman but not too bright."

At the time of the Judiciary Act, three circuit courts were created. (Today there are twelve, including one for the District of Columbia.) The Eastern circuit covered Connecticut, Massachusetts, New Hampshire, and New York; Rhode Island and Vermont were added when they joined the Union. The Middle circuit contained Delaware, Maryland, New Jersey, Pennsylvania, and Virginia. The Southern circuit consisted of South Carolina and Georgia, adding North Carolina when it joined the Union. To save expenses at the time, the circuit courts did not have their own judges. Instead, each district judge sat in the circuit court when it met in his state. In addition, two Supreme Court judges joined them, traveling by horseback, or "riding the circuit," to each region.

At the top of the pyramid is the U.S. Supreme Court, the highest legal authority in the land. In 1789, it was staffed by five associate judges and one chief justice. Today, there are eight associates and a chief justice. In general, the Supreme Court does not hear trial cases. In those cases, judge and jury try to determine whether a crime has been committed or if a person is guilty. Instead, the Supreme Court reviews cases from the circuit court level and can accept cases from federal courts or state supreme courts where the decisions are based on an issue of federal law.

The Judiciary Act of 1801 was passed on February 13, less than three weeks before the expiration of the last Congress ever controlled by the Federalists. (They ceased to function as a political party by 1817.) Although it did clear up some cumbersome organizational difficulties, such as no longer requiring Supreme Court judges to travel all over the countryside, it was obviously an attempt to pack the courts. That meant the Federalists were trying to put as many Federalist-thinking judges on the bench as possible. In that way, the Federalists believed they could keep control of the legal system. They thought that judges who were Federalists themselves would be less likely to strike down Federalist-sponsored laws. This reasoning still motivates modern presidents' appointments to the bench. A president from the Republican party, for instance, is likely to appoint a judge to the high court who holds Republican views.

The 1801 act also reduced the number of justices on the Supreme Court from six to five; when the next vacancy occurred, it would not be filled. The Constitution does not stipulate the number of justices on the Supreme Court. It says only that:

> The judicial Power of the United States, shall be vested in one supreme Court, and in such inferior Courts as the Congress may from time to time ordain and establish. The Judges both of the supreme and inferior Courts, shall hold their Offices during good Behaviour, and shall, at stated Times, receive for their Services, a Compensation, which shall not be diminished during their Continuance in Office.

In addition to altering the Supreme Court, the Judiciary Act of 1801 created six new circuit courts. That allowed Adams to appoint sixteen new circuit court judges. Because they were appointed at practically the last minutes of his presidency, they have been called the

Midnight Judges, which came to be a derisive term. The new act also gave Adams the power to appoint a number of justices of the peace for the new District of Columbia. On his final night in the White House, Adams named the last of forty-two new justices of the peace for the sparsely settled region. One of the commissions was intended for William Marbury. Believing he was truly saving the country, John Adams was relieved that at least the courts would be beyond the control of the incoming president.

After finishing his work that evening, Adams ordered the commissions to be carried over to the State Department. There, John Marshall, then acting as secretary of state, was waiting to authenticate them with the Great Seal of the United States and dispatch them to the various appointees that very evening.

Ironically, the man who would make the final decision in the case of *Marbury* v. *Madison* might be said to have started it all. No one knows exactly what happened that night, but although the commissions were all affixed with the Great Seal, they were not all delivered. Marshall later cited the chaos of the evening for the error. He simply ran out of time to deliver them. One of the judges who did not receive his appointment was William Marbury.

THE NEW PRESIDENT

Unlike most U.S. presidents, it can be said that Thomas Jefferson's greatest contribution to his country took place before he entered the White House. In 1776, as war with Great Britain neared, Jefferson was largely

T H E *G. Washington*

FEDERALIST:

A COLLECTION

O F

E S S A Y S,

WRITTEN IN FAVOUR OF THE

NEW CONSTITUTION,

AS AGREED UPON BY THE FEDERAL CONVENTION,
SEPTEMBER 17, 1787.

IN TWO VOLUMES.

VOL. II.

NEW-YORK:

PRINTED AND SOLD BY J. AND A. M'LEAN,
No. 41, HANOVER-SQUARE.
M, DCC, LXXXVIII.

THOMAS JEFFERSON, THE INCOMING PRESIDENT, WAS STAUNCHLY OPPOSED
TO THE VIEWS ESPOUSED IN *THE FEDERALIST*, A COLLECTION OF ESSAYS THAT
CONSTITUTED THE PHILOSOPHY OF THE FIRST TWO PRESIDENTS.

responsible for the magnificent oath to freedom called the Declaration of Independence. It is one of the most important of all American documents.

After writing the declaration, Jefferson was governor of Virginia during the Revolution, a member of the Continental Congress in 1783, and minister to France, which put him out of the country when the Constitution was drafted. He came home in 1789 as Washington's secretary of state and then became an unwilling vice president under Adams.

But Jefferson was in a mood to be friendly and conciliatory to Adams and to all the opposition on the morning of his inauguration as third president of the United States, March 4, 1801. The new president's feelings of compromise did not last, however. It was not long before he discovered how thoroughly Adams had packed the judiciary. He called what the former president had done "an outrage on decency" and later modified that by declaring, "I can say with truth that one act of Mr. Adams' life, and one only, ever gave me a moment's personal displeasure. I did consider his last appointments to office as personally unkind." Actually, Jefferson was most unhappy about the prospect of beginning his administration with the courts so stacked against him and his party, possibly rendering his decisions and actions useless.

Soon after he learned about the issuance of many new commissions, Jefferson also found out that some of them had not been delivered. In one of his first presidential decisions, he stopped all future deliveries, which was easy because they had apparently been left on the desk in the State Department. With James Madison, his new secretary of state, still en route to the capital, Jefferson asked Attorney General Levi Lincoln to commission a new slate of justices. He reduced the number and, in a spirit of fairness, he did not appoint all Republicans but reappointed some from the list Adams had drawn up. Then Jefferson told Lincoln to deliver the new commissions to the designated appointees.

Marbury and Madison

One judge who did not receive a new commission from Jefferson was William Marbury. For a person who was a central figure in a historic U.S. court case, very little is known about him. Marbury was forty-one years old at the time of the lawsuit and originally from Annapolis, Maryland. He had been in the nation's capital for some time serving as an aide to Federalist Benjamin Stoddert, first secretary of the navy, which is presumably why Adams issued him a commission. Beyond that, the main thing known about William Marbury is that he obviously was a man determined to get his new job.

The man named in the lawsuit by Marbury was James Madison, who would become the nation's fourth president in 1809 but was now Jefferson's newly appointed secretary of state. A fellow Virginian whose ideas formed a large part of the final Constitution, he was also a personal friend. Like Jefferson, Madison had been formally educated, but unlike Jefferson, he was sent out of the Virginia colony to the College of New Jersey (now Princeton University).

Madison served four terms in the House of Representatives before Jefferson chose him as secretary of state. He was a scholarly man with a brilliant mind, but he was not a particularly skilled politician. Madison believed in individual liberties and states' rights but also tried to balance them with a strong federal government. As secretary of state, Madison, not Jefferson, was named in the suit by Marbury. It was the job of the secretary of state to deliver the commissions, which, under orders of President Jefferson, Madison had refused to do.

THE MATTER GOES TO COURT

In all probability, Madison would have been unable to deliver Marbury's commission with or without presidential order, because it is likely that Jefferson had the original commissions destroyed. For a time after the initial refusal, nothing much happened. Then when the new Congress met in December 1801, Jefferson urged the repeal of the Judiciary Act of 1801 in his message to the legislative body. Actually, he did not use the word "repeal." Perhaps feeling he could persuade Congress by not acting in too forceful a manner, he just waltzed around the subject. Instead of an outright appeal, Jefferson suggested that, "The judiciary system of the United States, and especially that portion of it recently erected [meaning the Act of 1801], will of course present itself to the contemplation of Congress."

Also in December, William Marbury, still without his commission, took legal action along with Dennis Ramsay, Robert Townsend Hooe, and William Harper. Their lawyer, Charles Lee, had been the U.S. attorney general under both Washington and Adams. He was also the brother of Revolutionary War hero Henry (Lighthorse Harry) Lee. After Madison refused to deliver the commissions, Charles Lee invoked the "original jurisdiction of the United States Supreme Court." The Supreme Court hears very few original jurisdiction cases; that is, cases in which it would be the first court to hear a lawsuit. Most original jurisdiction cases are heard in district courts. However, in *Marbury* v. *Madison*, the Supreme Court would be acting much as a trial court.

The petition from Marbury and the others also called for a *writ of mandamus* to be issued to Madison, which was done. A writ of mandamus was originally a formal order issued by the British crown to command a person to perform an official act specified within the duties of his office. It later came to mean a judicial order from the bench on behalf of those who were affected by the failure of an official to perform a legal duty. It is not awarded as a matter of right but at the discretion of the court. The writ is usually not issued until all other alternatives have been investigated. In modern American law, mandamus is generally issued by a superior court directing a lower court to perform an act, such as hearing a certain case that the lower court has refused to hear.

Meanwhile, Congress did indeed contemplate what Jefferson called an unconstitutional law, meaning the Judiciary Act of 1801. On January 6, 1802, John Breckinridge of Kentucky introduced a repeal bill in the Senate. After some squabbling, it was passed there by a vote of 16 to 15 and then in the House by a much larger majority. The repeal effectively cancelled the jobs of the circuit judges Adams had appointed.

The Federalists immediately countered with a claim that the repeal law was unconstitutional because the circuit judges had been appointed for life. Indeed, fearing that the Federalist-dominated Court would declare just that, the Congress countered with a bold maneuver. It quickly passed a bill that simply abolished the upcoming June term of the Court, setting the next session to begin the second Monday of February 1803. Now the Federalists were truly alarmed; such action to them was tampering with the fundamental independence of the judiciary.

Jefferson was pleased with postponing the next Supreme Court term. After receiving the writ of mandamus from Marbury and the others, John Marshall, now chief justice of the Supreme Court, issued an order to Madison, directing him to show why a writ should not be delivered. Pushing the next Court term forward by a few months gave the president more time to deal with the problem.

One way Jefferson dealt with it was simply to ignore the Court order. When Marbury went to see Madison about the commission, he was told to see the clerk, Jacob Wagner, who said it was not in the files of the State Department. This further annoyed Marbury, who now asked the U.S. Senate for help. With the influence of a friendly senator, a motion was introduced that would compel Madison to show what had happened to the undelivered nominations. A fierce debate followed, and the motion was defeated. But by this time, everyone on both sides of the issue was fuming at everyone else.

Finally, on February 9, 1803, the Supreme Court met to deal with the case of *Marbury* v. *Madison*. By this time, the legal issues were fueled by temper and disharmony on both sides. A relatively small disagreement between a man seeking a job and an employer who refused to give it had now become a matter of great moment in the history of the United States. It was a moment that would reverberate through time.

Congress of the United States,

begun and held at the City of New York,

on Wednesday the fourth of March one thousand seven hundred and eighty nine.

THE Conventions of a number of the States having, at the time of their adopting the Constitution, expressed a desire, in order to prevent misconstruction or abuse of its powers, that further declaratory and restrictive Clauses should be added: And as extending the ground of public confidence in the Government, will best insure the beneficent ends of its Institution—

RESOLVED by the Senate and House of Representatives of the United States of America in Congress assembled, two thirds of both Houses concurring, that the following Articles be proposed to the Legislatures of the several States, as Amendments to the Constitution of the United States, all, or any of which Articles when ratified by three fourths of the said Legislatures, to be valid to all intents and purposes, as part of the said Constitution; viz.

ARTICLES in addition to, and Amendment of the Constitution of the United States of America, proposed by Congress, and ratified by the Legislatures of the several States, pursuant to the fifth Article of the original Constitution.

Article the First... After the first enumeration required by the first article of the Constitution, there shall be one Representative for every thirty thousand, until the number shall amount to one hundred, after which the proportion shall be so regulated by Congress, that there shall be not less than one hundred Representatives, nor less than one Representative for every forty thousand persons, until the number of Representatives shall amount to two hundred, after which the proportion shall be so regulated by Congress, that there shall not be less than two hundred Representatives, nor more than one Representative for every fifty thousand persons.

Article the Second... No law varying the compensation for the services of the Senators and Representatives, shall take effect, until an election of Representatives shall have intervened.

Article the Third... Congress shall make no law respecting an establishment of religion, or prohibiting the free exercise thereof; or abridging the freedom of speech, or of the press, or the right of the people peaceably to assemble, and to petition the Government for a redress of grievances.

Article the Fourth... A well regulated Militia, being necessary to the security of a free State, the right of the people to keep and bear Arms, shall not be infringed.

Article the Fifth... No Soldier shall, in time of peace be quartered in any house, without the consent of the Owner, nor in time of war, but in a manner to be prescribed by law.

Article the Sixth... The right of the people to be secure in their persons, houses, papers, and effects, against unreasonable searches and seizures, shall not be violated, and no warrants shall issue, but upon probable cause, supported by oath or affirmation, and particularly describing the place to be searched, and the persons or things to be seized.

Article the Seventh... No person shall be held to answer for a capital, or otherwise infamous crime, unless on a presentment or indictment of a Grand Jury, except in cases arising in the land or naval forces, or in the Militia, when in actual service in time of War or public danger; nor shall any person be subject for the same offence to be twice put in jeopardy of life or limb; nor shall be compelled in any criminal case to be a witness against himself, nor be deprived of life, liberty, or property, without due process of law; nor shall private property be taken for public use, without just compensation.

Article the Eighth... In all criminal prosecutions, the accused shall enjoy the right to a speedy and public trial, by an impartial jury of the State and district wherein the crime shall have been committed, which district shall have been previously ascertained by law, and to be informed of the nature and cause of the accusation; to be confronted with the witnesses against him; to have compulsory process for obtaining witnesses in his favor, and to have the assistance of counsel for his defence.

Article the Ninth... In suits at common law, where the value in controversy shall exceed twenty dollars, the right of trial by jury shall be preserved, and no fact tried by a Jury, shall be otherwise re-examined in any Court of the United States, than according to the rules of the common law.

Article the Tenth... Excessive bail shall not be required, nor excessive fines imposed, nor cruel and unusual punishments inflicted.

Article the Eleventh... The enumeration in the Constitution, of certain rights, shall not be construed to deny or disparage others retained by the people.

Article the Twelfth... The powers not delegated to the United States by the Constitution, nor prohibited by it to the States, are reserved to the States respectively, or to the people.

ATTEST,

Frederick Augustus Muhlenberg, Speaker of the House of Representatives.

John Adams, Vice President of the United States, and President of the Senate.

John Beckley, Clerk of the House of Representatives.

Sam. A. Otis, Secretary of the Senate.

AT THE TIME OF *MADISON V. MARBURY*, THE CONSTITUION AND ITS AMENDMENTS WERE FAR MORE POWERFUL IN CREATING THE LAW OF THE LAND THAN ANY DECISIONS MADE BY THE SUPREME COURT.

TWO
THE CHARACTER OF THE COURT

CHIEF JUSTICE JOHN MARSHALL was operating under a distinct disadvantage at the onset of *Marbury* v. *Madison*. The disadvantage was the lack of power of the U.S. Supreme Court. Far from the respected old institution it is today, the Court had little prestige and not much authority in the early 1800s because the leaders who framed the Constitution had some doubts about a strong judiciary. They blamed the courts of Great Britain for much of what they considered unfair treatment of the colonies. So, when they drew up the Constitution, they wanted to ensure strong executive and legislative branches, but they were not ready to give equal power to the judiciary.

A YOUNG COURT IN A YOUNG NATION
Until the time of *Marbury* v. *Madison*, the Supreme Court had heard only a few cases each year, and none of them had much importance. Marshall actually thought he might have some free time on the Court to write a biography of George Washington. This lack of a prominent place for the judiciary began back in 1787, when leaders met at the Constitutional Convention in Philadelphia. All the delegates agreed that there had to be some kind of legal system to enforce the laws that the

new government would create. But some of the delegates wanted to keep power in the states. They were suspicious about creating any kind of national judiciary. Others were equally determined to create a system that would not only enforce national law but would take precedence over state law as well.

These strong stands on both sides resulted in Article III of the U.S. Constitution. It did create a Supreme Court and it did give that Court both original and appellate jurisdiction, meaning the right to try cases as a trial court and to review cases from lower courts. However, it also said that the Court was subject to "such Exceptions and under such Regulations" that the Congress might decide to make. That hardly placed the Supreme Court on an equal footing with Congress. Articles I and II of the Constitution—which create Congress and the office of president—are far more detailed in duties and responsibilities than Article III, which deals with the judiciary. More details were added when Congress passed the Judiciary Act of 1789, which created the three-tiered legal pyramid structure and created six judgeships for the Supreme Court.

Given the disagreement over the function and power of the legal system, it is probably not surprising that most Americans had little regard for the Supreme Court during the early years. Even George Washington had some trouble finding six good men who were willing to take the job. He finally did persuade statesman John Jay to become the first chief justice, but Jay soon grew disgusted with the lack of power and prestige of the Court and got out as soon as he could.

Even when all the grand plans for the new capital city of Washington were being drawn, no one thought of

THE *MARBURY* CASE TOOK PLACE AT A TIME WHEN THE NATION BARELY EXISTED AS WE KNOW IT TODAY. IN THIS UNDATED ILLUSTRATION, THOMAS JEFFERSON AND JAMES MADISON DISCUSS THE SITE OF THE NATION'S FUTURE CAPITAL.

WHEN THE UNITED STATES BEGAN, THE SUPREME COURT WAS CONSIDERED OF SO LITTLE IMPORTANCE IT DIDN'T EVEN HAVE ITS OWN BUILDING. UNTIL 1810, THE JUSTICES WORKED OUT OF A FIRST FLOOR COMMITTEE ROOM IN THE CAPITOL BUILDING.

housing the Supreme Court. Until 1810, the justices worked out of a first floor committee room in the Capitol building. When the Capitol was fully functioning, they were given some cramped rooms in the basement. (The Supreme Court did not get its own home in the nation's capital for decades; the cornerstone of the Supreme Court Building was laid in 1932 and it was completed in 1935.)

DEFINING ITS ROLE

In a sense, during those first few years leading up to *Marbury* v. *Madison*, the Supreme Court was inventing itself, trying to define its role in conjunction with the executive and legislative branches of government. The first meeting of the newly created Supreme Court was on February 2, 1790, in what had been the Royal Exchange building in New York City, then the nation's capital. It was not much of a meeting because there were no cases for the Court to hear. So they all went home. The next few sessions, the longest lasting ten days, were devoted to setting rules and establishing ways to admit lawyers to practice before the high Court.

One of the earliest decisions was *Hayburn's Case* (1792), which involved the Court's judicial function. Congress passed a law that year authorizing the U.S. circuit courts to hear claims for disability pensions by veterans of the Revolution. At the time, five of the six justices on the Court—John Jay, William Cushing, James Wilson, John Blair, and James Iredell—were also judges on three circuit courts. They refused to serve as arbiters of pension claims because they said that would impose a nonjudicial duty on the Court, which would violate the separation of powers. Congress changed the claims

THE PATH TO THE SUPREME COURT, THEN AND NOW

The U.S. Supreme Court in the twenty-first century receives appeals to hear some 4,000 cases each year. That is far more than John Marshall could have imagined and far more than the Supreme Court can actually take on. In fact, the modern Court hears only about two hundred appeal cases yearly. The modern Court also wrestles with issues that would have been foreign to Marshall. Yet, in many ways John Marshall would still recognize the Supreme Court, for it maintains many of its traditions. Quill pens made from goose feathers are still in use. A seamstress is still employed full time to mend the justices's robes. Justices still announce their decisions publicly but agree to them in private.

As in Marshall's day, most of the cases that reach the Court are petitions asking for a review of a decision by a lower court—a federal district or state appeals court. In Marshall's time, however, the Court was required to hear all appeals; today, there are far too many so the Court has to choose. Most of the appeals are filed by attorneys, but any citizen can ask the Supreme Court to hear a case.

Since the Judiciary Act of 1925, the justices are required to select only the cases they feel are important. Since nine justices cannot possibly read all the appeals, that job is given to the Court clerks. They summarize the cases and present them to the justices, who hold a conference to decide which ones to accept.

Once the Court says yes to a case, it sends for the case records held in the lower court. A hearing is scheduled.

usually about two or three months ahead. On the day that the lawyers from opposing sides present their oral arguments, the nine justices sit on a high bench in the courtroom looking down on the attorneys. It is a great honor to present an oral argument before the U.S. Supreme Court, but it can also be a frightening process.

Usually, each side gets half an hour to present the case, and a huge hanging clock in back of the chief justice's chair lets the lawyer know when time is up. When the red light goes on, the attorney stops talking.

After the cases have been presented, the justices meet on Wednesdays and Fridays to discuss them. These conferences are held in complete secrecy. No one but the nine justices are in the room, and no one knows exactly what is said except the justices themselves. Privacy is guarded as jealously as in Marshall's day.

The decision of the Supreme Court is formally announced several weeks later from the same courtroom where the oral arguments were heard. Thanks in large part to Marshall, all the justices no longer read aloud their dissenting or concurring opinions. When the case has been decided, the Court gives its majority opinion and a dissenting opinion or opinions if there are any. Copies are made and the decision is published in the *United States Reports*.

procedure at the next session. This was not a case that made much news, but it can be seen as an early attempt by the federal judiciary to refuse to enforce what it regarded as an unconstitutional law.

Chisholm v. *Georgia* (1793) was the Supreme Court's first instance of flexing its authority over the states. The case presented to the nation's leaders a conflict of special interests: federal jurisdiction and state sovereignty.

The executors for the estate of a South Carolina merchant, Alexander Chisholm, sued the state of Georgia for the value of clothing that was supplied to it by the merchant during the Revolution. The executors had first tried to find a Georgia court to take the case, but all refused on the grounds that a state was sovereign and could not be sued by citizens of another state. So the case went to the federal court. The state of Georgia, which did not even send a representative to court, claimed once again that it could not be sued because it was sovereign and independent. By a vote of 4 to 1, the Supreme Court declared that sovereignty belonged to the people of the United States in order to form a Union, and Georgia was not a sovereign state in that Union.

The Court's decision made a number of legislators highly nervous at the thought of creditors suddenly descending upon the federal courts. To most, it seriously undermined states' rights. That led to the rather speedy ratification of the Eleventh Amendment to the Constitution on February 7, 1795. It said, in effect, that a state cannot be sued by the citizens of another state or by a foreign country. For the first time, a decision of the Supreme Court had been overturned by a constitutional amendment.

However, the Supreme Court refused to back down

on another case that involved the issue of state power. Many British creditors had brought cases to recover money that was owed to them by Americans before the Revolution. The Treaty of Paris (1783) at the end of the Revolution authorized the debts to be paid. But the state of Virginia passed its own law that allowed its citizens to pay off any debts owed to British citizens by giving the money to the state treasury. In *Ware* v. *Hylton* (1796), the Court voided the Virginia law by a vote of 4 to 0. It said that the Treaty of Paris nullified any Virginia state law. That was the only case John Marshall, then an attorney in Virginia, ever argued—and lost—before the Supreme Court.

Still in the process of finding itself, the Supreme Court took on a case that involved constitutional limitations on government power in *Calder* v. *Bull* (1798). Caleb Bull and his wife, beneficiaries in the will of Norman Morrison, were denied the inheritance by a Connecticut court. They tried to appeal but were told that more than eighteen months had passed, so the appeal was denied. However, the Bulls got the state of Connecticut to change the restriction and let them appeal the ruling. The Calders, who were the original heirs, declared that the state's action violated Article I, Section 10 of the Constitution, which prohibits ex post facto laws (made after the fact).

The Court was unanimous that the Connecticut legislation was not an ex post facto law. It said that Section 10 referred to criminal law, not civil disputes. This decision by the Court has been attacked through the years because it limited the ex post facto law to criminal statutes.

When the high Court, with John Marshall presiding, took on the case of *Marbury* v. *Madison*, it had a history of some ten years of significant decisions behind it. But nothing had really defined and secured the place of the judiciary in the government of the United States. Was it merely a necessary but weaker third branch, or was it one of three equal partners in governing the nation? *Marbury* v. *Madison*, sometimes called the Supreme Court's most important decision, established once and for all the role of the Court as an equal partner in the federal government.

THE *Marbury* JUSTICES

Besides their duties on the high bench, the justices of the Supreme Court also served as circuit court judges at the time. That meant they had to travel a good deal in a specified geographical area, or circuit. When the members of the Court met in Washington, D.C., they had to put up with a city still under construction and without many comforts. This home of the federal government at the time included Georgetown on the northern side of the Potomac River and Alexandria on the southern side. The President's House, as the White House was then called, looked little like the classic structure it is today. It stood on Pennsylvania Avenue about a mile from the Capitol, which had only a north wing; the center and south wing would be added years later. The roads were merely dirt lanes that allowed coaches to get in and out of the city.

In Washington, the justices lived together in an old boardinghouse. It was said that they had an interesting tradition when they gathered; supposedly, they drank wine only if the weather was bad. If that were true, it would not have been as restricting as it sounds. According to the *Smithsonian*, Marshall would sometimes tell the other judges, "Our jurisdiction extends over so large a territory that the doctrine of chances makes it certain that it must be raining somewhere."

Other reports, however, say that the justices also enjoyed a glass of port wine after dinner and when discussing cases after they had heard the oral arguments.

Samuel Chase (1741–1811) was born in Princess Anne, Maryland. He signed the Declaration of Independence and joined the Court at the request of Washington in 1796. Now nearly sixty years old and an able lawyer, he was suffering from gout and was known for his noticeably coarse manner. During the early struggles between the Federalists and the Jeffersonian Republicans, Chase's legal decisions were highly political and pro-Federalist. For Chase, politics always came before his judicial duties. For example, as he was on the way to preside at the trial of James T. Callendar, a pro-Jefferson writer who had made some nasty remarks in print about Adams, Chase remarked, "It is a pity that they had not hanged the rascal." This outraged President Jefferson, who later charged him with improper actions on the bench and giving a political address to a grand jury. That led to his impeachment trial by the Senate. In March 1805, the Senate, which was acting as a trial court, found him not guilty. His acquittal clarified the provision in Article III, Section I of the Constitution that seated judges can be removed only for criminal acts. In other words, they hold the office as long as they exhibit "good behavior."

William Cushing (1732–1810) of Scituate, Massachusetts, was the first man appointed to the U.S. Supreme Court and, at age sixty-seven, the oldest on the bench at the time. A Harvard graduate and a lawyer, his most notable act came while serving as chief justice of the supreme judicial court of his native state. Cushing ruled in 1783 that the "all men are born free and equal" clause in the state bill of rights abolished slavery in Massachusetts. Washington appointed him to the Court shortly after it

Associate Justice Samuel Chase may have been appointed to the bench because of his strong support of the Federalist philosophy that Chief Justice Marshall espoused.

was formed in 1789. Cushing, a modest man with an elegant manner of speaking, turned down the chief justice spot in 1796 because of poor health but stayed on the bench until his death.

Alfred Moore (1755–1810) was from New Hanover County, North Carolina, and an officer in the American Revolution. He returned home to manage the family plantation but entered politics in 1782 as attorney general of his home state. After serving a term in the state legislature, Moore went back to private practice. Elected a judge in the North Carolina Superior Court in 1798, he was appointed to the bench by Adams the following year. Moore, who was the same age as Marshall, had little influence on the Court and left only one recorded opinion during his tenure. In *Bas* v. *Tingy* (1800), he upheld the view of France as an "enemy" nation during the undeclared naval war of 1798–1799. Moore retired due to poor health in 1804.

William Paterson (1745–1806) emigrated from County Antrim, Ireland, in 1747 and was one of the framers of the U.S. Constitution. A graduate of the College of New Jersey, he was one of the state's first two senators and its governor for four years (1790–1793), after which he joined the Court. The city of Paterson, New Jersey, and William Paterson University in Wayne, New Jersey, are named for him. He was one of the most scholarly of American judges, with an outgoing, friendly personality that put people at ease.

Bushrod Washington (1762–1829) was born in Westmoreland County, Virginia, and graduated from William and Mary College, Williamsburg, Virginia, where he was an original member of the Phi Beta Kappa honor society. George Washington was his uncle. The younger Washington served in the Continental Army and studied law in Philadelphia. Adams put him on the Court in 1798. When George and Martha Washington died, Bushrod inherited their home, Mount Vernon. He also encouraged Marshall to write his five-volume biography, *The Life of George Washington* (1804–1807). Washington was the youngest of the judges and the one Marshall knew best. His great strength was the patience and fairness he demonstrated when riding circuit, especially in some of the politically charged jury trials of the day. Although judged naive on almost any other subject, Washington was genuinely interested in the law.

John Marshall, Chief Justice

As the chief justice of the U.S. Supreme Court, John Marshall combined a brilliant mind with an unpolished personality. He is arguably America's most important judicial figure.

Marshall grew up in the backwoods of Virginia, where he was born in a log cabin in Germantown, Prince William County, on September 24, 1755. He was the first of fifteen children born to Thomas and Mary Randolph Keith Marshall. It was not unusual to have large families in colonial days, but it was indeed unusual for all of the children to live to adulthood, which the Marshall children did. Marshall's father was a surveyor and a friend of George Washington's. When grown, Marshall always referred to his father with affection. As he said in his *Autobiographical Sketch*, his father was "a far abler man than any of his sons" and "the solid foundation of all my success." When John was a young man and the family had moved to the Blue Ridge Mountains, the elder Marshall became a member of the House of Burgesses, the ruling body of the colony in Williamsburg.

CHIEF JUSTICE JOHN MARSHALL HAD TO RECTIFY A HUGE DISADVANTAGE—WHEN HE WAS APPOINTED, THE COURT HAD FAR LESS POWER THAN THE EXECUTIVE AND LEGISLATIVE BRANCHES OF THE GOVERNMENT.

A year in boarding school at Campbelltown Academy and a few months at the College of William and Mary in 1780, where he attended law lectures, was the extent of Marshall's formal education. That was not unusual for the time and place, however. Few of Virginia's young men of the period—Thomas Jefferson and James Madison being notable exceptions—were formally educated.

Marshall was barely nineteen when war began between England and the colonies. He became a lieutenant in the Fauquier County militia and then in the Continental Army. He saw action at Brandywine Creek, at Germantown near Philadelphia, and at Valley Forge. It was during the harsh winter at Valley Forge that Marshall's lifelong admiration for George Washington began.

Marshall was ordered back to Virginia in late 1779 to command a yet-unformed army of troops to defend the Carolinas. But money for the defense was never raised, so he had some time off to study law at the College of William and Mary. Those three months of Marshall's full formal study of the law were short but meaningful. He learned from one of the most respected lawyers in the country, George Wythe. Probably the first great American law teacher, Wythe also taught Thomas Jefferson. Wythe had served in the Continental Congress and signed the Declaration of Independence. He was appointed to the High Court of Chancery and the Court of Appeals. His purpose was to form leaders as well as lawyers.

In 1783, Marshall married Mary Willis Ambler (called Polly). Although she suffered from bouts of depression, the couple remained devoted to each other throughout the fifty years of their married life. Marshall set up a law practice in Richmond, Virginia. He had been admitted to the bar in 1780.

THE FAMILY AND SOCIAL MAN

Throughout his lifetime, Marshall's friends and colleagues marveled at the chief justice's devotion to his wife. A semi-invalid given to bouts of depression, Polly Marshall appeared to most to be a lonely, unhappy woman. But it is said that the two shared a happy marriage and the ability to laugh together. Their children were strictly raised, especially to be quiet around the house because of their mother's precarious health. But as adults, they remembered Marshall as an affectionate, proud father.

Even though much of his time was devoted to law, Marshall was very involved in the social life of Richmond, Virginia. He and Polly enjoyed entertaining. He loved to invite guests in for good food and fine spirits, mint juleps being a favorite. He was a visitor to the local racetrack and a member of the Barbecue Club, where lawyers, bankers, and businessmen met to discuss the events of the time.

IN 1783, JOHN MARSHALL MARRIED MARY WILLIS AMBLER, KNOWN AS POLLY. THOUGH SHE WAS A SEMI-INVALID, THEIR MARRIAGE WAS LONG AND HAPPY, AND MAY HAVE SUSTAINED HIM THROUGH PROFESSIONAL WOES.

PRESIDENT JOHN ADAMS NAMED JOHN MARSHALL SECRETARY OF
STATE IN 1800, BUT HIS STAY IN THAT POSITION WAS SHORT-LIVED
BECAUSE ADAMS LOST THE NEXT ELECTION.

Marshall was admitted to practice before the Court of Appeals in 1785 and would argue about a hundred cases before the court through the 1790s. These years only enhanced his growing reputation and stature. However, he lost his first case before the appeals court, *Hite* v. *Fairfax*, a dispute over land grants, in 1786. Most of the rest of his career was far more successful.

TO THE CABINET

In 1797, John Marshall was one of three ministers sent to France by President Adams to negotiate a commercial agreement with France to protect U.S. shipping. The undertaking very nearly plunged the two countries into war and became known as the X, Y, Z Affair. Once Marshall and the other ministers arrived in Paris, French agents (called X, Y, and Z in official correspondence) suggested that a bribe of $250,000 be paid to Charles-Maurice de Talleyrand, the French foreign minister, in addition to a loan of $10 million, before negotiations could even begin. When word of the suggested bribe reached the United States, there was a great public outcry. The American ministers refused to pay. The incident was peacefully settled by the Convention of 1800, and Marshall returned home in 1802.

Praised for his diplomacy, Marshall was offered a seat on the Supreme Court to fill the vacancy left by James Wilson. But Marshall wanted to continue his legal career, so he declined the president's offer and Bushrod Washington took the appointment. However, George Washington then persuaded Marshall to run for the House of Representatives. When the Sixth Congress met in December 1799, it was Marshall's sad duty to announce the death of the nation's first president.

Washington died on December 4 at his home in Mount Vernon, Virginia, at the age of sixty-seven.

Marshall's congressional term was short. In May 1800, Adams named him secretary of state without even consulting him. Marshall wanted to stay in Congress, but he accepted the job and performed well. He almost had to, for Adams soon left the capital for a few months to go home to Braintree where his beloved wife Abigail was ill. That left Marshall, as Adams's most trusted colleague, pretty much in charge of the administration. Abigail recovered and Adams returned. But Marshall's post as secretary of state was short-lived, too.

John Adams lost the election of 1800, and now the federal government was no longer Marshall's concern. With a new administration coming in, he intended to go home to his wife and family in Virginia and practice law.

Marshall did return to his Virginia home, but he never went back to practice law. That autumn, Chief Justice Oliver Ellsworth had resigned because of his health. Adams wanted to put another Federalist in the high seat before Jefferson took office. But Associate Justice Cushing was too old for the position. Adams thought about appointing the younger Paterson but believed that might insult Cushing. Instead, he asked John Jay to come back, but Jay refused because he thought that the country had too little respect for its highest legal authority. After Jay refused, Adams apparently asked Marshall if he had any ideas on a potential candidate. Marshall suggested that the president might want to reconsider the appointment of Paterson, but Adams said no. So it happened that on January 18, 1801, Adams nominated forty-five-year-old John Marshall to be chief justice of the Supreme Court.

THREE
DEBATING THE ISSUES

JOHN MARSHALL, the country boy from Virginia, was now the highest legal authority in the land. He had accepted the appointment with this letter to Adams:

> *I pray you to accept my grateful acknowledgements for the honor conferred on me in appointing me Chief Justice of the United States.*
>
> *This additional and flattering mark of your good opinion has made an impression on me which time will not efface.*
>
> *I shall enter immediately on the duties of the office and hope never to give you occasion to regret having made this appointment. With the most respectful attachment, I am Sir your Obedt. Servt. J. Marshall.*

As for Adams, even though Marshall was the fourth choice for the job, the president would speak of the appointment as one of the best political acts of his career. In fact, he said, "My gift of John Marshall to the people of the United States was the proudest act of my life." But that was years later. At the time, the appointment merely

MARSHALL

JOHN MARSHALL,

Chief Justice of the U.S. 1801

When John Marshall was first nominated for the position of chief justice, legislators were slow to approve it. They feared his independence, and perhaps they were right, since he changed the nature of the Supreme Court.

solved a political problem for Adams. Yet the president, being a lawyer himself, knew a good lawyer when he heard one. Marshall's loyalty to the Federalists and to Adams himself were factors, too.

THE CONFIRMATION

Now the Senate had to confirm the nomination, which came after the 1800 election, but before Jefferson and the new Republican majority in the legislature took office. Marshall came to the bench with excellent experience in the law, legislative matters, and politics. Although he was to be a Federalist in a Jeffersonian-Republican government, it would seem that President Adams could not have made a better choice. Even so, the legislators did not unanimously accept the nomination at first. Some members thought Marshall was just too independent for the high court. But most of the opposition came from those who were shocked that William Paterson had not been nominated. Paterson had many friends in the Senate. Wrote Senator Jonathan Dayton, a Federalist, to Paterson, "With grief, astonishment & almost indignation, I hasten to inform you, that, contrary to the hopes and expectations of us all, the President has this morning nominated Gen. Marshall. . . . "

However, even before Marshall was confirmed, Paterson sent him a letter of congratulations and went out of his way to praise him. Paterson wrote in a reply to Dayton that Marshall "is a man of genius, of strong reasoning powers, and a sound, correct lawyer."

Feeling was so strong in the Senate that voting on the nomination was suspended for a week. The senators hoped that the president, hearing of their reluctance over the choice, would change his mind. But Adams did not. Therefore, on January 27, 1800, the Senate confirmed John Marshall as the new chief justice of the U.S. Supreme Court. The vote was unanimous. In a return letter to Paterson, Dayton explained why all the senators voted for Marshall when there had been so much initial opposition. Dayton pointed out that they were aware that Adams opposed the nomination of Paterson and there was, therefore, little likelihood of his being chosen. They were also aware that any animosity toward Marshall existed not because of his record but simply because the senators had preferred Paterson. Once confirmed, the salary for the new chief justice was $4,000, about $56,000 in today's money. (More than two hundred years later, the chief justice makes $192,000 annually; associate justices are paid $184,000.)

A Federalist, Marshall was about to face a Jeffersonian-Republican-dominated Congress. He did, however, want to maintain a cordial relationship with the new president, even though they were obvious political enemies. Jefferson seemed to want that, too. Two days before the inaugural, Jefferson sent Marshall a letter asking him to deliver the presidential oath and adding that he would be there on time. Marshall replied that he would be pleased to deliver the oath and he would make it a point to be on time, too. Even while trying to maintain a cordial relationship, Marshall clearly intended to do what he could in his position to preserve Federalism. As he wrote on the morning of Jefferson's inauguration, "Of the importance of the judiciary at all times, but more especially the present I am very fully impressed. I shall endeavor in the new office to which I am called not to disappoint my friends."

MARSHALL ON AND OFF THE BENCH

It is said that Chief Justice John Marshall was the same in manner and appearance whether at his home in Richmond or walking the halls of Congress in Washington, D.C. He would as quickly bend down to have a game of marbles with a neighborhood boy as stop for a chat with a distinguished senator. If he arrived at the courtroom ahead of time, he would often sit among the waiting lawyers and talk as though he were one of them, which indeed he had been. But once court began and Marshall sat upon the bench in his capacity as chief justice, wearing his judicial robes, he was transformed. The dignity and the kind look were still there, but now he was a man of firm intent and grave manner, interested only in the matter before him.

Jefferson's inaugural speech, delivered to a crowded Senate chamber, was memorable, although many in the room could not hear it. Public speaking was not one of the new president's strong points. However, Marshall was impressed by his appeal for national unity. Jefferson spoke of the nation as being all Republicans and all Federalists and asked for support for his administration.

At the end of the address, Marshall delivered the oath of office to the third president. For that moment, it seemed as though these two political enemies might find a common ground for the good of the country.

THE JUDICIARY ACTS OF 1789 AND 1801

The case of *Marbury* v. *Madison* was the first to overturn a law passed by Congress. But it grew out of the Judiciary Acts of Congress in 1789 and 1801.

After a good deal of spirited debate, the framers of the U.S. Constitution in 1787 had decided on three branches of national government. In addition to the executive and legislative branches (the president and the Congress), they created a national court system, or judiciary. This corrected an omission in the Articles of Confederation (1781–1789) that had been governing the new country since it gained independence from Great Britain. The articles had not provided for a judiciary at all.

The U.S. Constitution goes into great detail concerning the executive and legislative branches, but gives the judiciary only the barest of outlines. So it fell to the Congress of the new nation to give a specific form to the structure of the courts.

This was not an easy task. The new government was weak. Sensitive to wrongs suffered when English courts governed the colonies, everyone had a different idea about how the new judiciary should operate. The back-and-forth arguments went on through the entire first session of Congress. Finally, there was an agreement. Most felt it was workable if temporary, that it could serve as a framework until something more durable could be devised. Instead, as Kermit Hall comments in his work on the Supreme Court, "The Judiciary Act of 1789 ranks as one of the most important enactments Congress has ever undertaken, more akin to a constitutive act (like amendments to the Constitution) than to ordinary legislation." And in fact, its major point—the three-tiered federal judiciary—remains in effect today.

The Federalist Congress passed the Judiciary Act of 1801 before the Jeffersonian Republicans could take office. Since the 1789 law, the Federalists had wanted to expand the organization and jurisdiction of the national courts it created. Now faced with losing the executive office and Congress to an opposed political faction, the Federalist-controlled Congress passed the Judiciary Act of 1801 before Jefferson was sworn in.

A year later, the Repeal Act was passed, which restored the former judicial system. But Congress also enacted the Judiciary Act of 1802, which postponed the next session of the Court until the following February. So the deposed circuit judges did not get their jobs back anyway.

THE MARSHALL COURT

Chief justices can shape the character of their courts and such was the case with John Marshall. He was sworn in on February 4, 1801, on a rainy winter morning in Washington, D.C. The other justices present were

ASSOCIATE JUSTICE WILLIAM CUSHING WAS THE OLDEST MEMBER OF THE
MARSHALL COURT.

Chase, Cushing, and Washington. The press took little notice of the event, illustrating the rather low regard in which the judiciary was held. In fact, the Court did very little business that month.

As Supreme Courts go, the Marshall Court was young, with Cushing the only justice in his sixties and boyish-looking Bushrod Washington only age thirty-eight. The justices came from various parts of the Union. The room where the Marshall Court first met was under the south end of the House of Representatives quarters. It had two windows, and was heated by a fireplace. It was not quite finished and rather sparsely furnished. The bench where the justices sat was not raised as is the custom in courtrooms today.

Because Marshall was free from circuit duties his first year on the Court, he had a chance to think about his position as chief justice. It was clear from the beginning that he would remain silent on public affairs, which was a change from much judicial practice of the time. Marshall never voiced an opinion on how his colleagues or predecessors acted. Whatever the reasons for his silence, he set a precedent for others in his position to follow, that of being above the rough and tumble of politics.

The changes in the Marshall Court began almost immediately. He introduced changes because he believed that the court system had to be a powerful voice. His new practices and procedures started the judiciary on its way to becoming the equal partner in government that it is today. For instance, before his appointment, it was the custom for each justice to deliver his own opinion on each significant case. That was the procedure in the English courts. However, in as young a court system as that of the United States, six delivered opinions, even if they all agreed, did not give an impression of overall authority and power. Under Marshall, the justices united behind a single opinion, which was new in judicial history. If any of the justices disagreed with the majority opinion, he could write a dissenting opinion, but this was exceedingly rare throughout the nineteenth century. In fact, Marshall was so concerned with unanimous opinions and with the legitimacy of the Court that he often delivered the opinion for the Court even if he disagreed with it.

THE MIDNIGHT JUDGE

It is somewhat ironic that all the fuss over Marbury and his commission began with the appointment of the so-called Midnight Judges. For the chief justice of the Supreme Court was something of a Midnight Judge himself. Marshall had been the secretary of state when the about-to-depart John Adams put him in the highest seat on the Court mere weeks before Jefferson took office. Marshall was put there for essentially the same reason the Midnight Judges were appointed—to keep Jefferson from nominating members of his own party.

Marshall was still secretary of state when he was nominated for the Court, but Adams asked him to stay on in that position until a successor was appointed. None was, so Marshall actually held two jobs until Jefferson took over. (He was only paid for his court job, however.) In fact, Marshall was busy at work as secretary of state on the night the Marbury commission was supposed to have been delivered. The problems that followed led to a worsening political climate and then to the case of *Marbury* v. *Madison*.

jefferson and marshall

Into this atmosphere of discord between two political factions was the very real and active animosity between President Jefferson and Chief Justice Marshall. A Marshall biographer quotes the chief justice speaking many years after *Madison* v. *Marbury*: "I have never believed firmly in [Mr. Jefferson's] infallibility. I have never thought him a particularly wise, sound and practical statesman [and] I have not changed this mode of thinking." According to the same biographer, Jefferson had this to say of his relationship with the chief justice: "when conversing with Marshall, I never admit anything. . . . So sure as you admit any position to be good, no matter how remote from the conclusion he seeks to establish, you are gone. . . . Why, if he were to ask me if it were daylight or not, I'd reply, 'Sir, I don't know, I can't tell.'"

The dislike shared by both men is ironic in that they were so alike in many ways. They were both highly intelligent, able politicians who were trained as lawyers. They shared a Virginia culture and background. They were intensely and unashamedly patriotic. And, on a lighter note, neither seemed to take any notice of his personal appearance. It is said that Jefferson often wore old slippers while conducting official business and was on occasion mistaken for a servant by those entering the White House.

As for Marshall, his reputation for not knowing how to dress was almost as well known as his reputation for being a fine lawyer. No matter how refined his manner became, no matter what position he held, Marshall never seemed to get the knack of wearing clothes in style. However, he was so well liked that cartoons of the day took good-natured jibes at his generally sloppy appearance. One cartoon in his pre-Supreme Court days showed him arguing a case while wearing torn knee breeches and a vest with a hole in it. According to one story, a prospective client was so disturbed when Marshall arrived with his shirt hanging out of his pants that the man hired another lawyer who wore proper attire, which at the time was a white wig and a black suit. But at the courthouse while the man was waiting for his trial, he watched Marshall at work on another case. He promptly asked Marshall to become his lawyer again but said he could only pay him five dollars because he had already paid another lawyer. Marshall agreed and won the case.

The relationship between Jefferson and Marshall was about to become more intense than ever. Marshall took a first step toward their disagreement over *Marbury* when he and the associate justices met in their small room in December 1801. They granted a preliminary motion that would show cause why a writ of mandamus should not be delivered to Madison. The writ would direct him to deliver the commissions to Marbury and the others. Some in the Senate, notably John Breckinridge and Stevens Thomson Mason of Virginia, saw the Court's action of issuing the writ as a direct attack on Jefferson. They also thought it was the Court's way of delaying repeal of the judiciary act and was, therefore, a threat against Congress.

Interestingly, the Supreme Court chose a day in the

next term to hear the *Marbury* case, but the next term was nullified by Congress. So the Court did not meet again to take up the matter until February 1803. In that interim, thirty justices of the peace had been commissioned and were at work in the District of Columbia. It would almost seem that the *Marbury* matter was already settled. However, *Marbury* v. *Madison* went far beyond the scope of undelivered commissions. At the outset of the trial, Marshall may not have meant to use it to establish the authority of the Court, but as the case unfolded his fears about legislative power and the Court's role doubtless increased.

The discord between the legislature and the Supreme Court caused fireworks even before the trial actually opened. Marbury petitioned Congress for a copy of its hearings about the matter of commissions, saying he had no other way to show proof that he had been awarded a commission at all. The Republicans in charge of Congress voted it down, saying that it was just a trick to show authority over the president.

Throughout the young life of the new nation, the Supreme Court was regarded as by far the weakest of the three branches of the government. Despite the system of checks and balances set up in the Constitution to ensure that one branch did not overpower the other, the Court had never been the slightest threat to the autonomy of either the president or the Congress. Now, into the charged and angry political atmosphere of 1803, the case of *Marbury* v. *Madison* came to the U.S. Supreme Court.

Attorney Charles Lee argued William Marbury's case in front of the
Supreme Court.

four

MARSHALL'S BRILLIANCE: THE DECISION

AT THE OUTSET, *Marbury* v. *Madison* had little to suggest it would become perhaps the most important court case in U.S. history. Even those directly involved did not seem overly interested. Court opened on Monday, February 7, 1803, although arguments did not begin until February 10. Justice Paterson did not show up until February 11, and Justice Moore arrived late on February 12. Cushing missed the entire proceedings because he was ill. President Jefferson and Secretary of State Madison were preoccupied with an enormous land purchase from France. Even the Federalists had shifted their attack on Jefferson to his foreign policy. As for John Marshall, he missed the opening day of court, although he often did so. Travel at the time was not a very exact science, and it was not always possible to arrive on a certain day. However, for the chief justice, this case would answer what he considered the vital question in the government of the United States of America: Who was the final authority on what is and is not the law?

THE ARGUMENTS

In the case of *Marbury* v. *Madison*, the justices sat as a trial court rather than as an appellate court reviewing a case from a lower court, as had previously been the case. Marbury's request for a writ of mandamus was not an appeal from a lower court but an original action brought before the Supreme Court itself. Marbury and his associates had to demonstrate why the writ of mandamus ordering the commissions should be delivered.

Each side was given the opportunity to argue its case before the Court. Charles Lee represented Marbury and Attorney General Levi Lincoln represented Madison. But Lincoln would respond only to written questions, and Madison was not even present. He had simply not responded to the Court order—an obvious insult to judicial authority.

Lee's job was to prove that the commissions for Marbury and the others had been completed by Adams and Marshall. He also wanted to show that the Court had the authority to order Madison to issue them. He opened the argument by stating that Marbury's commission was valid and that he had the right to receive it. In addition, Lee said that the Court was within its right to order Madison to deliver Marbury's commission according to the Judiciary Act of 1789, Section 13, which says a writ of mandamus may be issued "in cases warranted by the principles and usages of law, to any courts appointed, or persons holding office, under the authority of the United States."

Lee summoned two State Department clerks, Jacob Wagner and Daniel Brent, to testify. They objected, saying they were not bound to release any information about the State Department. But Lee argued that they were public servants as well as agents of the president and they should testify about public matters. Marshall agreed. The clerks told the Court details of what had happened in the White House and State Department on the night of March 3, 1801. However, they said they did not know what had become of the actual commissions.

Now, Lee called Attorney General Levi Lincoln. He did not want to testify either. As acting secretary of state, he was the president's principal deputy. But he was also the nation's attorney general. Lincoln said he would answer questions if the Court said he must, but he asked that Lee put them in writing so Lincoln could have the time to study them.

Marshall agreed. As biographer Jean Smith observed, "It was apparent from the interchange between Marshall and Lincoln that each was doing his utmost to prevent the issue from escalating into a full-blown confrontation between the executive branch and the Court. Lincoln deferred to the Court's authority. Marshall made it plain that the court would respect executive privilege."

The session ended, and the Court met again the next day, February 11. Lincoln testified that he did not know what happened to the commissions. He said he had seen them and that they were sealed with the Great Seal of the United States, but he could not say for sure whether any had been made out to Marbury, Ramsay, or Hooe.

As a last piece of evidence, Lee offered a document signed by Marshall's brother, James. It stated that he had seen the commissions in the secretary of state's office, had been unable to deliver them, and had returned them to the State Department. In his final argument, Lee said that the Court had the power to issue the writ to the secretary of state because Congress gave it the power to do so in the Judiciary Act of 1801. After that, Lee gave his closing argument.

As was customary, now was the time for response from the opposing side, for in this case the Supreme

Court was acting as a trial court. But when asked, Lincoln said Madison had given him no instructions and so he had nothing to say. This disturbed Marshall as he did not want the proceedings to seem biased or unfair to any side. He had expected Lincoln to make a response.

THE OPINION

John Marshall had a problem. Of utmost importance to him was the integrity of the U.S. court system. But the Court was faced with a serious dilemma. If it decided in favor of awarding Marbury his writ of mandamus—thereby ordering Madison to deliver the commission—President Jefferson would certainly tell his secretary of state to ignore the order. Such an action would challenge the authority of the Court and weaken its already tenuous power.

In addition, Jefferson had grown extremely popular with the people by this time. Defying him might even start impeachment proceedings against Marshall. There were already impending impeachment hearings against Justice Chase. Such an action against the chief justice would certainly do the Supreme Court—and Marshall—no good.

However, if the Court denied Marbury his writ, it would look as though the justices had acted out of fear of the president. Whatever the decision, the supremacy of the law would be denied and the Court would be placed in a position inferior to the executive branch. These were things Marshall could not tolerate. Yet it seemed that whatever decision he made would end in disaster. The fact that Marshall himself had originally failed to deliver the commissions, and thereby had basically brought on the disaster, merely made things worse.

Over the next ten days, Marshall deliberated, came to a conclusion, and persuaded his fellow justices. The latter presumably would not have been too difficult. Paterson and Moore had missed part of the proceedings anyway. Washington was generally willing to follow Marshall's direction, and Cushing was absent. As for Chase, the Republican Congress was impeaching him for partisan behavior and he was uncharacteristically quiet.

On February 24, Marshall delivered his decision, speaking for the united Court. With the intellectual awareness and clarity of reasoning that marked his career, he had found an elegant legal solution. It gave something to both sides and established the power of judicial review that exists in the U.S. court system today.

Yes, said Marshall in a speech delivered from the bench that lasted nearly four hours, Marbury was entitled to his commission. It had been approved by the Senate and signed by the president. Yes, said Marshall, Marbury was entitled to a remedy for the wrong that had been done to him. But would that wrong be rectified by the writ of mandamus ordering the commission to be delivered? No, said Marshall. The writ was issued because of Section 13 of the Judiciary Act of 1789, and Marshall declared that section to be unconstitutional. Therefore, the Court did not have the power to issue the writ.

Section 13 of the Judiciary Act of 1789 begins by stating that the "Supreme Court shall have exclusive jurisdiction of all controversies of a civil nature, where a state is a party, except between a state and its citizens, and except also between a state and citizens of other states, or aliens, in which latter case it shall have original but not exclusive jurisdiction." It goes on to discuss jurisdiction of suits against ambassadors and other public officials. The specific part that Marshall noted as unconstitutional as it pertains to *Marbury* v. *Madison* is the last sentence:

> The Supreme Court shall also have appellate jurisdiction from the circuit courts and courts of the several states, in the cases herein after specially provided for; and shall have power to issue writs of prohibition to the district courts, when proceeding as courts of admiralty and maritime jurisdiction, and writs of mandamus, in cases warranted by the principles and usages of law, to any courts appointed, or persons holding office, under the authority of the United States.

Section 13 of the act gave the Supreme Court the power to issue writs of mandamus. Therefore, it gave the Court original jurisdiction, which refers to the starting place (or court) of a case. The act allowed someone to go directly to the Supreme Court for a writ of mandamus without first going to a lower court. However, the U.S. Constitution grants original jurisdiction to the Supreme Court in only two instances: cases that involve ambassadors and public ministers and those involving differences between two states, such as one suing another for money owed. Therefore, Marshall saw a conflict between Section 13 of the act and the Constitution. Giving original jurisdiction regarding writs of mandamus was, Marshall reasoned, granting the Court powers not given by the U.S. Constitution.

Marshall declared Section 13 unconstitutional because it enlarged the original jurisdiction of the Court contained in Article III. A nation's law should depend upon the Constitution, said Marshall, not be altered by Congress as a matter of political will. The Court had the power to declare Section 13 unconstitutional because judges take an oath of upholding the Constitution, which is the supreme law of the land. As the supreme law, it triumphs over mere legislation. The conclusion, argued Marshall, was that the Court did not have the power to order Madison to deliver Marbury's commission.

Marshall delivered the Court's opinion with solemn authority, as though speaking to the American people themselves. He spoke of the relationship between citizens and their Constitution, a document so important that it must never be trifled with. He reminded the American people that the entire fabric of their government had been built upon the Constitution. He said that there was no middle ground between the Constitution as supreme law or as just another legislative act. If it is supreme law, then it is superior to acts of the legislature. To regard it as otherwise, said Marshall, is to reduce the written Constitution to nothingness.

Moving on to the next logical step, Marshall pointed out that in a case where a law is in conflict with the Constitution, the Court has no choice but to declare a conflicting law unconstitutional. It was not that the Supreme Court was so wise in such matters; it was simply that the justices had taken an oath to uphold the supreme law.

In his long decision speech directed at the American people, Marshall very much wanted to make it clear that a legislative act in violation of the Constitution could not be tolerated. He said, "Thus, the particular phraseology of the Constitution of the United States confirms and strengthens the principle, supposed to be essential in all written constitutions, that a law repugnant to the constitution is void; and that *courts*, as well as other departments, are bound by that instrument."

With one decision, Marshall had converted a no-win situation into victory. He had acknowledged the right of Marbury to ask for his commission. But instead of challenging the president, Marshall had deemed the Court powerless to deliver the commission because Section 13 of the Judiciary Act was unconstitutional. In so doing, he established the authority of the U.S. Supreme Court to declare an act of Congress unconstitutional. It became, and continues to be, the law of the land.

Had Marshall not confirmed the power of judicial review for the high Court at that time, some argue that it might never have been confirmed. The next case involving the Court's power to declare a law unconstitutional did not happen until 1857 with *Scott* v. *Sandford*. After so many years of not questioning the supremacy of congressional laws, it might have been impossible to break that precedent.

Marshall was not the first American to state that the Constitution is the fundamental law and that it must be preferred over congressional laws. It had actually been a part of the American legal tradition dating from colonial and revolutionary experiences. James Otis, a political activist from Massachusetts, helped to write the colonists' grievances against the British government in the 1760s. His famous challenge came in 1761 against the writs of assistance that allowed the British to search any house for smuggled goods. Otis cited the doctrine of natural law underlying the rights of citizens to declare that even writs authorized by the British Parliament were null and void.

Most of the framers of the Constitution believed in the Constitution as fundamental law. Alexander

Hamilton wrote about it in *The Federalist*. Other supporters of judicial review included Chancellor James Kent (1763–1847), who wrote extensively of the U.S. Constitution and the federal system in *Commentaries on American Law*, four volumes published from 1826–1830.

THe AFTermaTH

Today, Americans generally take for granted that the Supreme Court has the last word on the Constitution. Few challenge the Court's right in this matter. Instead, each administration, if it has the opportunity, tries to put justices on the Court who favor its political point of view.

The Supreme Court had not attained that status in 1803. *Marbury* v. *Madison* was a defining moment in the legal life of the nation. Marshall's brilliant decision changed the power of the Supreme Court of the United States and altered its history, but it was hardly noticed. It was little talked about in legal areas outside of Washington, D.C. News items or the text of the decision were printed in the press of the largest cities, including the *Aurora*, a pro-Jefferson newspaper in Philadelphia. Like the president, the publishers of the newspaper were at first pleased with the decision. The paper applauded the Court's independence and dramatically declared, "The weight of your authority then calmed the tumult of faction, and you stood, as you must continue to stand, a star of the first magnitude."

But in general, Marshall had just asserted the supremacy of the Court in matters of the Constitution. No one seemed to care. Nor did many challenge it. Neither house of Congress offered one word of criticism. Marshall's reasoning was not questioned, nor was the authority of the Court to overturn an act of Congress.

Though the Supreme Court had asserted that the

Constitution is the fundamental law of the land, both laws and the Constitution can be changed. The U.S. Constitution has been altered many times since *Marbury v. Madison*, through the passage of amendments.

At first, the president and the Republicans were pleased: Marbury was, after all, out of a job. (Marbury's name lives on in history books but the man himself faded into historical obscurity. According to records, he became president of a Georgetown bank in 1814 and died, still without a commission, in 1835.) It was not long, however, before Jefferson became agitated over the outcome. Mostly, he feared that the Court would now go on a spree of declaring laws unconstitutional, especially those just passed by the Republican-controlled Congress. Besides, Jefferson had a constitutional worry of his own. He was engaged at the time in negotiations with France over the Louisiana Purchase. For less than three cents an acre, the United States could buy the 828,000 square miles that the French owned in North America. That made up the western half of the Mississippi River basin.

The Louisiana Purchase, signed on May 2, 1803, was the greatest land bargain in U.S. history, but Jefferson was not sure it was legal. The Constitution says nothing about acquiring new land. In the end, the best way to handle the constitutionality issue was simply to ignore it. Congress quietly approved the purchase, Jefferson quietly signed it, no one objected, and the United States doubled in size.

Grounds for Dismissal

John Marshall was passionate in his delivery of the *Marbury* opinion because he was passionate about the independence of the judiciary. But now, even though he

FOR LESS THAN THREE CENTS AN ACRE, PRESIDENT THOMAS JEFFERSON BOUGHT 828,000 SQUARE MILES OF LAND FROM THE FRENCH. THE COURT, AS WELL AS CONGRESS, QUIETLY APPROVED.

PRESIDENT THOMAS JEFFERSON SIGNED THE LOUISIANA PURCHASE TREATY
ON APRIL 30, 1803. THIS DOUBLED THE SIZE OF THE UNITED STATES.

was relieved by the outcome, he still feared for the future of the nation's court system. Marshall knew well that Jefferson and the Republicans were looking for ways either to intimidate or remove Federalist judges from the bench. If they were successful, Marshall also knew that the seats would not be filled with Federalist sympathizers. The independence of the high Court would disappear in subservience to the Republicans.

Even before the outcome of *Marbury*, the Republicans had begun to take bold steps toward removing judges. They did so because they had been absolutely certain the *Marbury* case would be decided against them. Madison would be ordered to deliver the commissions and the Republicans would then charge partisanship on the Court, thereby perhaps removing a judge or two. But that was not the way it worked out.

At first, however, the Republicans were successful in their impeachment efforts. They impeached John Pickering, judge of the U.S. Court for the district of New Hampshire. He was found guilty of drunkenness and profanity while on the bench. Pickering was also mentally ill and totally incapable of holding office. The Senate did not factor in his mental illness and convicted him of the charges in March 1804.

That was followed in 1805 by the trial of Samuel Chase, who was presented with eight articles of impeachment, including anything that anyone had ever complained about concerning him. Most court watchers thought he would be removed from office. Chase spoke for three hours in his own defense. He was acquitted on all counts, and Marshall was greatly relieved. He had earlier written to his brother that these impeachments threatened a pure, independent judiciary. Marshall also had a very real fear about his successor should he himself be impeached. He knew

THE BURR TRIAL

In 1807, Marshall presided at one of the most spectacular cases in U.S. history, the trial of Aaron Burr. Jefferson threw all his presidential might behind a conviction for treason. Marshall wanted to balance what was right for society with what was right for the individual. He showed once again that his interest was in the law, not

Burr had killed Alexander Hamilton in a duel in 1804. After the impeachment trial of Supreme Court Justice Samuel Chase, he fled to Philadelphia to avoid arrest in two states. He and a friend, General James Wilkinson, planned an invasion of Mexico to establish an independent government. Burr spoke of severing the western part of the United States and apparently proposed to the British minister that in exchange for gold, he would persuade Westerners to secede from the Union. He also made threats against Jefferson. Eventually, Burr was arrested, charged with treason, and tried before Marshall.

Historians have never been able to decide whether Burr was really serious in his talk of breaking off part of the country or whether it was all intended as a grand scheme to get money. Certainly, Burr faced financial disaster throughout his life, and he was forever coming up with get-rich-quick schemes that never worked. Whether this was just another such fancy is not known for sure. President Jefferson, however, was certain that Burr was guilty of treason.

Marshall and the Court decided the charge of treason was not proved. Burr was acquitted but lived the rest of his life under suspicion. He could never quite live down his past. After the trial he went to Europe where he tried vainly to get Napoleon's assistance in a plan to conquer Florida. In need of money once again, he returned to New York City four years later, where he practiced law until his death in 1836.

No one benefitted from the Burr case. Not Burr, nor the president, whose liberal reputation was tarnished because of his overt animosity toward Burr. Even Marshall did not escape. Such was the popular feeling against Burr that Marshall was denounced in the press and accused of partisan behavior.

that Jefferson would appoint Spencer Roane of Virginia as
the next chief justice. The president had Roane waiting in
the wings to appoint him on the impending death of Justice
Ellsworth. But Ellsworth had resigned, which allowed
Adams to appoint Marshall. Should Marshall go, Roane
would enter the Court. And with Roane on the Court,
Marshall knew that all his theories of an independent
judiciary would vanish. Legal historian R. Kent Newmyer
wrote that Marshall believed Roane assumed that "the
Supreme Court was a creature of the national government,
when it was in reality the creation of the written constitution, which emanated from the American people in
solemn convention."

But with the acquittal of Chase, as Albert Beveridge
noted in his four-volume biography of Marshall,

> For the first time since his appointment, John
> Marshall was secure as head of the Supreme
> Bench. For the first time since Jefferson's elec-
> tion, the National Judiciary was, for a period,
> rendered independent. For the first time in five
> years, the Federalist members of the Nation's
> highest tribunal could go about their duties with-
> out fear that upon them would fall the avenging
> blade of impeachment, . . . One of the few really
> great crises in American history had passed.

STUART V. LAIRD

The Repeal Act of 1802, which had restored the original
judiciary system, remained a point of contention in the
Congress until the high court finally heard the case of
Stuart v. Laird six days after the *Marbury* decision, on
March 2, 1803. It involved the constitutionality of the

repeal act. The Court voted 5 to 0; Marshall did not vote because he had earlier heard the case on the circuit court in Richmond.

Two constitutional questions were presented. Could Congress abolish the circuit courts created in 1801, thereby depriving judges of their jobs even though they had already been appointed and qualified on "good behavior"? And, could Congress force Supreme Court justices also to sit as circuit judges?

Paterson gave the Court's opinion, to which Marshall agreed. The answer was yes and yes. He said that Congress had the power to transfer a case that existed under the 1801 act to a case created under the repeal of 1802. As for the circuit judge requirement, it was simply too late, said the Court, to challenge a practice that had been going on for so long. Said Paterson, the question of the circuit courts that had so long been occupying the government "is at rest, and ought not now be disturbed."

What the Court did was to demonstrate that it would not become an instrument of politics between the two major parties. The Supreme Court under Marshall would base its weight and power on the legality of the Constitution.

FIVE
IN THE YEARS TO COME

THe real importance of Marshall's decision in the case of *Marbury* v. *Madison* is not so much what happened in 1803 but what has happened in subsequent years. The outcome of that case affected the lives of citizens throughout the nineteenth century, although most did not realize it, just as it affects the lives of those who live in the twenty-first. More than two hundred years after the decision, its outcome remains the law of the land. It has never been seriously challenged.

After *Marbury* v. *Madison*, Marshall's position on the Supreme Court was never again placed in jeopardy. The Court itself was held in much higher regard than before and would remain so until the trial of the slave Dred Scott in 1857, a decision regarded as perhaps the Court's worst and one that cost it great prestige for a couple of decades.

The Court adjourned for a year after the *Stuart* v. *Laird* decision. The atmosphere between Congress and the Court was unsettled. Jefferson seemed satisfied that Marshall had risen above partisanship in both the *Marbury* and *Stuart* cases. Besides, the president was up for reelection in 1804, so he was eager to keep matters calm with the Federalists.

Another challenge in the Court would not be in the Republicans' best interests. However, not all members of Jefferson's party were inclined to agree. Some radicals, such as John Randolph of Virginia, were not prepared to accept the judiciary as the third branch of the U.S. government. The separation of powers was still in the infant stage, and the atmosphere worried Marshall. As he went home to Richmond, he remarked to former secretary of the treasury Oliver Wolcott, "We have fallen upon evil times, and I do not clearly perceive a prospect of better."

Marshall's Principles

After *Marbury* v. *Madison*, John Marshall still had many years ahead of him as chief justice. He had elevated the U.S. Supreme Court to a place of equal standing with the other branches of government. Now he would spend the rest of his life safeguarding the Court against anyone who would deny its position as defender of the Constitution.

Until he retired in 1835, Marshall followed two fundamental principles on the Court: the courts must protect the individual against the massed powers of the government (in other words, an individual is entitled to life, liberty, and property), and the extent of federal authority over the states must be established.

Over the next few years, from 1810 until 1824, in the cases of *Fletcher* v. *Peck, Dartmouth College* v. *Woodward, McCullough* v. *Maryland,* and *Gibbons* v. *Ogden,* Marshall built his decisions on the foundations that had been laid in the *Marbury* ruling. Each of these cases established a constitutional basis for a strong national government over the states. As a result, each one strengthened the power of judicial review that had been established with *Marbury*.

In addition, by striking down state laws and regulations, these decisions helped to create a strong economic common market.

In 1810, the Marshall court heard the case of *Fletcher v. Peck*, a complicated issue involving lawful contracts. The case had been dragging on in the courts for fifteen years. It involved the Yazoo lands, some 35 million acres including most of Mississippi and Alabama. The Georgia legislature had sold the land to a syndicate for $500,000. It was later learned that some members of the legislature had shared in the profits of the deal. Georgia voters threw out the entire legislature. The newly elected legislature repealed the act that had allowed the sale and burned the original copy in a public square. However, many citizens had already bought Yazoo lands and now wanted their money back. One of the buyers, John Fletcher, brought a suit against the seller, John Peck.

Marshall's Court decided for the buyers. A contract is a contract, said Marshall; the motives of the original legislators were irrelevant. The state of Georgia had made a contract, and it could not now say it was null and void. Marshall was saying that when a state makes a contract, it is obliged to honor it.

Backers of states' rights were furious at Marshall once again. The issue was complex, and the decision seemed to protect unscrupulous investors as well as law-abiding ones. But Marshall believed that the rights and obligations of contracts were essential to democratic law. They were protected under the Constitution. Eventually, the U.S. Congress bought up the Yazoo lands for about $5 million and sold them again.

Another matter of states' rights came up in 1819

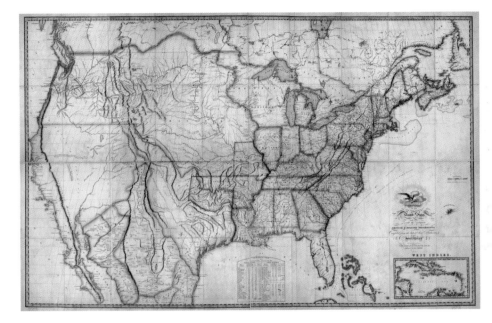

AMONG THE MANY CASES MARSHALL HEARD AFTER *MARBURY* WAS ONE INVOLVING THE YAZOO LANDS. THOUGH MANY FELT THE LEGISLATORS WHO SOLD THE LAND HAD ACTED IMPROPERLY, MARSHALL RULED THAT THE CONTRACT MUST BE HONORED WHATEVER THE SELLERS' MOTIVES.

with *Dartmouth College* v. *Woodward*. The college had been operating since 1769 under a charter by the British crown and was privately owned by a board of trustees. The newly elected Republican governor in New Hampshire and the Republican-dominated legislature wanted to get rid of the pro-Federalist Dartmouth board and elect a new board through the political process. It did so by enacting a statute that revised the royal charter and changed Dartmouth from a college to a university, which altered the process of internal control.

Lawyers for the college were led by Daniel Webster. He argued that the original charter was a contract and no state had the right to break it. Marshall and the Court agreed. According to Marshall, a state had no more right to break a contract with a corporation than it did with an individual. This had far-reaching implications. At this time, corporations were relatively new and untested business organizations in the United States. The Marshall decision kept them relatively free from interference by the state. As a result, by the end of the nineteenth century, corporations dominated the American economy.

Another 1819 case, *McCullough* v. *Maryland*, clearly established the distribution of powers between state and federal government. This asserted the all-important doctrine of implied powers; that is, powers granted *to* Congress in the Constitution even though they are not expressly given *by* the Constitution. It is regarded as one of Marshall's most important decisions and among his most eloquent. The specific issues involved were two: did the Congress have the power to incorporate a bank, and did a state have the right to tax an instrument of the federal government?

Congress chartered the Second Bank of the United

THE *DRED SCOTT* case

In a case begun in 1846 and settled by the Supreme Court in 1857, the slave Dred Scott sued his late master's wife for his freedom. Scott had been taken by Dr. John Emerson from the slave state of Missouri to live for a time in the free state of Illinois and in the Wisconsin Territory, which was also free. At similar earlier trials in Missouri, where the case was first heard, the courts had ruled that a slave was entitled to freedom by virtue of residence in a free state or territory—"once free, always free." After repeated delays, the U.S. Supreme Court, with Chief Justice Roger Brook Taney presiding, declared Scott to be a slave by a vote of 7 to 2. The Court ruled that: 1) Scott, although a citizen of Missouri, was not a citizen of the United States and therefore could not sue; 2) Scott was still a slave because he had never been free in the first place (Congress, said the Court, had no power to abolish slavery in territories); and, 3) the Missouri Compromise of 1820, which allowed for slave and free states, was unconstitutional. That was the second time the Supreme Court had declared a law passed by Congress to be unconstitutional.

States in 1816. Alexander Hamilton had created the First Bank in 1791 over the opposition of Jefferson and Madison, who said it was not authorized by the Constitution. Hamilton said it was loosely justified, so the bank was chartered for twenty years and then quietly expired. After the Second Bank was chartered, many Jeffersonians continued to oppose it on constitutional grounds. In fact, several states began to tax the bank's branches. Finally, in 1818, Maryland imposed a tax on all banks in the state that the legislature had not chartered. James McCullough, who was cashier at the Baltimore branch of the Second Bank of the United States, refused to pay.

The state of Maryland argued that the states had created the federal government and therefore the state was the authority in every matter not cited by the Constitution. That would include banking. But Marshall, speaking for the Court in a unanimous decision, thought otherwise.

First, the Court had to decide whether Congress had the right to establish a bank in the first place. The Constitution, Marshall declared, was not made by the states but by the people. And the Constitution contained only an outline of what power and structure belonged to the federal government. The most important powers were noted, but the rest had to be deduced. The creation of the bank by the federal government was justified because the Constitution had given it specific powers to tax and collect taxes, to borrow money, and to regulate commerce. Implied in these powers was the creation of a bank in order to carry out the specified duties. So, the Bank of the United States was constitutional. The doctrine of implied powers became a powerful force in the steady growth of federal government power.

The next question was whether a state, in this case the state of Maryland, had the right to tax a federal bank. Marshall said the Constitution and federal law were supreme. The power of a state to tax, important as that is, cannot supersede the powers of the federal government. In other words, a state cannot tax something over which it has no power. Declared Marshall, "the power to tax involves the power to destroy."

Significant as these decisions had been, Marshall was not through establishing the position of states' rights vis-à-vis the federal government. In 1824, the Marshall Court struck another blow to the states in the *Gibbons* v. *Ogden* decision. The Court ruled that states cannot interfere with congressional power to regulate commerce.

In 1807, New York gave Robert Fulton and Robert R. Livingston a monopoly on steamboat navigation in state waters because they built a boat that traveled the required speed—four miles an hour—up the Hudson River. In the following years, many challenged this monopoly. Aaron Ogden subsequently bought rights from Fulton and Livingston to operate steamboats between New York City and New Jersey. In 1819, he sued Thomas Gibbons, who was operating steamboats in the same waters with a federal license, but without purchasing rights from Fulton and Livingston. Ogden won the New York court case in 1820 and Gibbons appealed to the Supreme Court.

In a unanimous vote, Marshall's Court ruled for Gibbons. He defined commerce broadly, to include persons and even steamboats. Therefore, Gibbons' federal license took precedence over the New York State monopoly, which was created by a statute. This decision, although it was frequently explored again over the next quarter century, finally freed all navigation from monopoly control.

MARSHALL'S LAST YEARS

For most of his long years of service on the Supreme Court, Marshall was described as a generally contented man. His work was exhilarating to him, if frustrating and sometimes disappointing. Although he had always been in good health, early in 1831 he began to experience severe abdominal pains while covering his circuit duties in North Carolina. After several months of home remedies that did not work, he finally went to a doctor in Philadelphia, who diagnosed gallstones. Marshall underwent a successful operation in the fall of 1831 and appeared to make a rapid and complete recovery.

By November, he was thinking about returning to the Court, but his beloved Polly fell ill and by mid-December was confined to her bed. She died on Christmas day with Marshall at her bedside.

Marshall returned to Court duties, but his wife's death was a blow from which he never seemed to recover fully. He confided to friends that he wept for her every night.

After the Court term ended in 1835, Marshall was hurt in a stagecoach accident. He was also suffering from liver disease. Calmly and quietly, with his children at his bedside, Chief Justice Marshall died on July 6 at six o'clock in the evening. Only one of his children, his eldest son, Thomas, was not present. On the way to his father, Thomas had stopped for shelter in an abandoned building in Baltimore to escape a severe thunderstorm. The wind knocked a chimney into the dilapidated building, killing Thomas. Marshall was not told of his son's death.

The entire nation mourned the former chief justice's death and flags flew at half-staff. Even his political enemies voiced respect for his patriotism and integrity. The longest and most solemn procession Richmond had ever seen

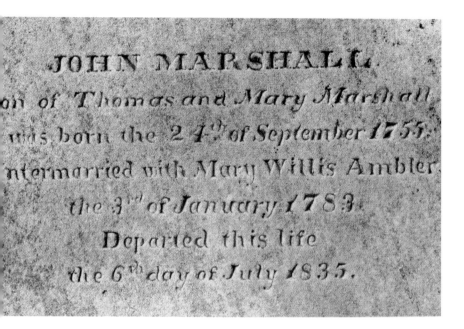

JOHN MARSHALL NEVER RECOVERED FROM HIS WIFE'S DEATH IN 1831. THEY ARE BURIED TOGETHER IN RICHMOND, VIRGINIA.

BUSHROD WASHINGTON HELPED MARSHALL WITH
HIS BIOGRAPHY OF WAHINGTON'S UNCLE GEORGE.

CHIEF JUSTICE JOHN MARSHALL SERVED ON THE
COURT UNTIL 1835. BESIDES DECIDING ON MANY
OTHER CASES, HE WROTE A FIVE-VOLUME BIOGRAPHY
OF GEORGE WASHINGTON. THIS PHOTOGRAPH SHOWS
HIS GLASSES AND PEN AND OTHER MATERIAL HE USED
FOR READING AND WRITING.

Marshall's Biography of Washington

Marshall began writing his biography of George Washington in 1801. The result—five volumes of about 3,200 pages—took five years to complete. It turned out to be more a history of the American people than the life of Washington, beginning with the early history of the British colonies and ending with the nation's first decade. The first president does not even appear as a character until volume two.

Although Marshall was an extremely disciplined man and used to hard work, writing the book was a challenge. But it was work he enjoyed; in addition, he and Bushrod Washington, who assisted him, expected the book to be a great success because of

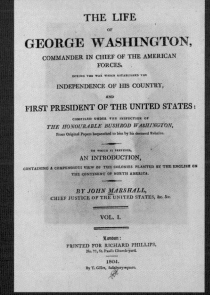

THE TITLE PAGE OF MARSHALL'S *THE LIFE OF GEORGE WASHINGTON*.

its subject. Bushrod estimated they would sell 30,000 copies at three dollars a book. Marshall planned to use his royalties to pay for the family's new home. Actually, only about 7,000 copies of the work were sold.

Marshall never seemed satisfied with the book and continued to revise it throughout his lifetime. Reviews of the book were mixed. Federalists loved it; Republicans were severe in their criticism.

wound through the city streets to honor him. Many words of praise were written in his honor, but perhaps his greatest eulogy was that at his death, the Constitution was firmly in place as the supreme law of the land.

Marshall is buried in Richmond next to Polly in Shockoe Cemetery. He had written his own epitaph for his tombstone, which can be seen today. This is the way he wished to be remembered:

John Marshall
Son of Thomas and Mary Marshall
was born on the 24th of September 1755
Intermarried with Mary Willis Ambler
the 3rd of January 1873
Departed this life
the sixth day of July 1835.

JUDICIAL REVIEW

Since *Marbury* v. *Madison*, there have been continuing battles between the Congress and the Court and the president and the Court. Thomas Jefferson was the first president to engage in battle with the high bench in *Marbury* v. *Madison*, but he was certainly not the last. One of the most notable cases occurred in 1935 between President Franklin D. Roosevelt and the Court led by Chief Justice Charles Evans Hughes.

Roosevelt, the only president to be elected to four terms, took office in 1933. The country was going through a devastating Depression. Thousands of people were out of work. Businesses collapsed, banks failed, and people lost their homes. Roosevelt was only the third Democrat to

TRADITIONS

The Supreme Court justices are very formal when it comes to seating. The chief justice always sits in the center of the courtroom bench. The senior associate sits to the right, the next senior to left, and so on. You can always tell the most junior justice; he or she is sitting in the farthest seat to the left of the chief justice.

Since 1880, justices shake hands with each other whenever they enter the courtroom.

It was always the tradition for justices to call each other "Mr. Justice." Since women are now on the court, however, they refer to themselves as "Justice (last name)."

After a Supreme Court justice retires, he or she gets to take home his chair from the courtroom or the conference room.

The traditional seal of the Supreme Court has a single star beneath the eagle's claws. The seal used by the present Court is the fifth one in the Court's history.

WHEN FRANKLIN DELANO ROOSEVELT BECAME PRESIDENT, HE PROPOSED THAT FOR EVERY JUDGE OVER THE AGE OF SEVENTY, HE WOULD APPOINT ANOTHER, YOUNGER JUDGE. THE IDEA WAS THAT HIS DEMOCRATIC APPOINTEES WOULD SUPPORT HIS ECONOMIC REFORMS, BUT CONGRESS DID NOT GO ALONG WITH WHAT BECAME KNOWN AS HIS "COURT-PACKING" PLAN.

enter the White House since the Civil War ended in 1865. He won in a landslide over incumbent Herbert Hoover with a promise of what he called a New Deal.

A short time after taking office, Roosevelt sent to Congress—and Congress passed—a series of economic laws that put people back to work, improved the economy and agriculture, and built highways and dams. In 1933, Congress passed the National Industrial Recovery Act (NIRA). It was the New Deal's major legislation, and it was wide-ranging. Among other things, the act declared a national emergency. It set up standards for work hours and minimum wages and fair competition rules for businesses.

The Supreme Court reviewed the New Deal in 1935 in *Schechter Poultry Corp.* v. *United States.* The case was rather minor. Slaughterhouse operators in Brooklyn had been found guilty of violating the new wage and hour provisions and "among other offenses, selling an 'unfit chicken.'"

The decision of the Court was unanimous. It struck down the government's program, mainly stating that the NIRA had given to the president the legislative power to make laws, which was against the Constitution.

Roosevelt was furious and accused the Court of being back in the horse-and-buggy days. He was not against judicial review in itself, he said, but he believed the Court was now abusing its power. Figuring he would have more trouble over future legislation with the Supreme Court, the majority of whom had been appointed by Republicans, the president had an idea. He proposed that for every justice on the Supreme Court age seventy or over, he would appoint another justice, up to a total of fifteen. This would not get rid of any justices now on the Court, but presumably because Roosevelt would appoint Democratic judges, he would then have a majority to pass his legislative package.

The president gave a speech to Congress in which he declared that additional justices would, in effect, save the Constitution from the actions of the Court. The idea, which became known as the "Court-packing" plan, did not work. Most members of Congress may not have liked the Court's decision, but they liked the idea of presidential interference with the high bench even less.

However, before the Senate could vote on the president's proposal, the Court—in its famous "switch-in-time-that-saved-nine"—voted to uphold other New Deal legislation. That contributed to the defeat of the "Court-packing" plan. It was a political blow to Roosevelt even though from then on he was able to get many other New Deal measures into law. He was able to get much notable reform legislation passed especially during his second administration. By 1939, the country was pulling out of the Great Depression and heading into World War II.

THE ALL-POWERFUL INFLUENCE

As arbiter of the Constitution, the Supreme Court has brought great changes to the nation. Operating within the law, justices can be traditionalists or activists or somewhere in the middle. Traditionalists go by the exact wording of the Constitution. They are said to have a narrow interpretation and will seldom reverse a previous Court decision. Activists are more inclined to think of what the words of the Constitution might imply in modern times. Their interpretation is said to be broad, and they are not loathe to break new ground.

The case of *Plessy* v. *Ferguson* (1896) is historically interesting because, although relatively insignificant at the time, the decision attained symbolic importance over the next six decades. The Court upheld a Louisiana statute that said a railroad had to provide separate but equal seating for blacks and whites. It was a test case to challenge the so-called Jim Crow laws the South passed to keep control of state governments in the hands of white voters. The Court's interpretation was that the Louisiana statute did not violate the Thirteenth and Fourteenth Amendments because requiring the races to be separate did not imply that one race was inferior.

Although presidents are often heard to say that they will put any qualified person on the Supreme Court, in reality they generally nominate justices of their own political party. They do so because they expect those people to look favorably upon legislation that the president favors, or at least to lean toward the president's philosophy of government. However, it does not always work out that way. President Dwight D. Eisenhower, a general, hero of World War II, and a Republican, was elected president in 1952. He nominated Earl Warren as chief justice. Warren had been a candidate for vice president on the Republican ticket in 1948. Most people expected him to be a traditionalist. But the Warren Court became the most activist yet seen in U.S. history. Its most famous decision occurred in 1954 in *Brown* v. *Board of Education*. The Court decided that the "separate but equal" policy that segregated U.S. schools was unconstitutional. The Warren Court's decision not only desegregated the American school system but opened the door to much civil rights legislation of the 1960s.

Under Chief Justice Warren Burger, the Supreme Court gave another controversial verdict in 1973 with *Roe v. Wade*, declaring that a Texas law prohibiting abortions except to save the life of a pregnant woman, was unconstitutional, broadly interpreting a constitutional right of privacy. Said the Court in a 7 to 2 decision, "the right to privacy or to personal authority in sexual matters, was fundamental under many controversial versions of liberal political theory." This decision broadened the Court's power by deducing a right not specifically stated in the Constitution.

Through the years, the Court has wrestled with controversial and challenging issues that affect the lives of all Americans. There is controversy over the constitutionality of death penalty laws. There are ever-increasing challenges to personal liberty and privacy. There is division over the jurisdiction of government to deny personal rights in order to thwart the actions of terrorists and other enemies of the nation. One time or another, the Supreme Court is likely to take up these matters because they concern the rights and liberties granted U.S. citizens by the Constitution.

Looking back, *Marbury* v. *Madison* was in itself a seemingly inconsequential matter. One man wanted a job that had been denied to him. Through circumstances and conflicting personalities of the time, the case became a turning point in defining the fundamental jurisdiction of the U.S. court system. Its outcome provided the Supreme Court with the power to declare acts of Congress unconstitutional. By implication, it could declare acts of the president unconstitutional as well if they exceeded the powers granted to the office. But above all, the outcome of *Marbury* declared the Court the final arbiter of the Constitution itself.

1787
Constitutional Convention creates a Supreme Court in
Article III of the Constitution

1789
Judiciary Act of 1789 establishes the structure of the
court system

1801
Judiciary Act of 1801 expands the court system

1802
Judiciary Act of 1801 is repealed

1803
Marshall establishes policy of judicial review in
Marbury v. *Madison*

1819
McCullough v. *Maryland* establishes federal government's
right to create a bank

1824
Gibbons v. Ogden establishes federal power to strike down
a state statute

1832
Worcester v. *Georgia* decreed that the Cherokee and other
Indian nations are independent political entities that
cannot be ruled by one of our states; this decision was
ignored by the federal government

1857
Scott v. *Sandford* denies freedom to a slave and declares Missouri Compromise of 1820 unconstitutional; raises public furor; called Court's worst decision

1886
Wabash, St. Louis & Pacific Railway Co. v. *Illinois* limits state power over railroads; leads to creation of Interstate Commerce Commission in 1887

1886
Presser v. *Illinois* held that the Second Amendment to the Constitution does not prohibit state governments from regulating an individual's ownership or use of guns

1896
Plessy v. *Ferguson* upholds "separate but equal" facilities in treatment of the races

1905
Lochner v. *New York* invalidates state law to regulate working hours; symbolized judicial misuse of power for decades

1919
Abrams v. *United States* upholds the right of the government to limit free speech and freedom of the press if they are intended to cause an illegal action or threaten national security

1937
Franklin D. Roosevelt fails in attempt to "pack the Court"

1943
Hirabayashi v. *United States* upholds federal decision placing curfews on Japanese Americans

1944
Korematsu v. *United States* justifies the relocation of Japanese Americans from their homes and imprisonment in "relocation centers" during World War II based on the needs of national security in times of crisis

1954
Brown v. *Board of Education* strikes down "separate but equal" laws; called the Court's most important decision of the twentieth century

1963
Gideon v. *Wainwright* establishes the guarantee of counsel to all defendants in criminal cases

1963
Abington School District v. *Schempp* determines that the government may not promote religion in public schools

1966
Miranda v. *Arizona* ruled that police must inform suspects in their custody that they have the right to remain silent and anything they say may be held against them, and that they have the right to consult a lawyer

1971
New York Times Co. v. *United States* upheld the freedom of the press

1973
Roe v. *Wade* establishes fundamental right to abortion

1978
Regents of the University of California v. *Bakke* denied the use of fixed quota based on race or ethnicity to justify university admissions

1990
Hodgson v. *Minnesota* allows states to impose greater limits on abortion rights

1992
Planned Parenthood of Southwestern Pennsylvania v. *Casey* determines that states have the right to impose burdens on access to abortion

2000
Bush v. *Gore* reverses the ruling of the Florida Supreme Court to allow a recount of state ballots in the national election for president

CHIEF JUSTICES OF THE SUPREME COURT

JUSTICE	Term	APPOINTED BY	NOTED FOR
John Jay	1789–1795	George Washington	Being first
John Rutledge	1795	Washington	Never confirmed
Oliver Ellsworth	1796–1800	Washington	
John Marshall	1801–1835	John Adams	*Marbury* v. *Madison*
Roger Brooke Taney	1836–1864	Andrew Jackson	Gave final decision in *Dred Scott* case, against Scott
Salmon P. Chase	1864–1873	Abraham Lincoln	Fairness in presiding over impeachment trial of President Andrew Johnson (acquitted)
Morrison Remick Waite	1874–1888	Ulysses S. Grant	
Melville Weston Fuller	1888–1910	Grover Cleveland	Declared federal income tax law unconstitutional in *Pollock* v. *Farmers' Loan and Trust Co.* (1894)

JUSTICE	TERM	APPOINTED BY	NOTED FOR
Edward Douglass White	1910–1921	William Howard Taft	Applied "rule of reason" to antitrust cases (1911)
William Howard Taft	1921–1930	Warren Harding	Only U.S. president to serve as chief justice
Charles Evans Hughes	1930–1941	Herbert Hoover	Led court through Roosevelt's New Deal legislation
Harlan Fiske Stone	1941–1946	Franklin Roosevelt	
Fred M. Vinson	1946–1953	Harry S. Truman	
Earl Warren	1953–1969	Dwight Eisenhower	Ended school segregation with *Brown* v. *Board of Education*
Warren E. Burger	1969–1986	Richard Nixon	Voted in *Roe* v. *Wade* for women's right to abortion (1973)
William H. Rehnquist	1986–	Ronald Reagan	

NOTES

Chapter 1

p. 17, John A. Garraty. "The Case of the Missing Commissions," *American Heritage*, June 1963, 14, no.4.

p. 25, U.S. Constitution, Article III, Section I.

p. 28, Garraty. "Missing Commissions."

p. 30, Dumas Malone. *Jefferson the President: First Term 1801–1805*. Boston: Little, Brown, 1970.

p. 31, Kermit L. Hall, ed. *The Oxford Companion to the Supreme Court of the United States*. New York: Oxford University Press, 1992.

Chapter 2

p. 44, Robert Wernick. "Chief Justice Marshall Takes the Law in Hand," *Smithsonian*, 1998, 29, no. 8.

p. 45, David Loth. *Chief Justice John Marshall and the Growth of the Republic*. New York: Greenwood, 1949.

p. 48, R. Kent Newmyer. *John Marshall and the Heroic Age of the Supreme Court*. Baton Rouge: Louisiana State University Press, 2001.

Chapter 3

p. 55, Jean Edward Smith. *John Marshall: Definer of a Nation.* New York: Holt, 1996.

p. 55, David Loth. *Chief Justice John Marshall and the Growth of the Republic.* New York: Greenwood, 1949.

p. 57, Bernard Schwartz. *A History of the Supreme Court.* New York: Oxford University Press, 1993.

p. 57, Schwartz. *History of the Supreme Court.*

p. 58, Smith. *John Marshall.*

p. 61, Kermit L. Hall, ed. *The Oxford Companion to the Supreme Court of the United States.* New York: Oxford University Press, 1992.

p. 65, Smith. *John Marshall.*

Chapter 4

p. 70, R. Kent Newmyer. *John Marshall and the Heroic Age of the Supreme Court.* Baton Rouge: Louisiana State University Press, 2001.

p. 71, Jean Edward Smith. *John Marshall: Definer of a Nation.* New York: Holt, 1996.

p. 73–74, Leonard Baker. *John Marshall: A Life in Law.* New York: Macmillan, 1974.

p. 75–76, Francis N. Stites. *John Marshall: Defender of the Constitution.* Boston: Little, Brown, 1981.

p. 77, Newmyer. *John Marshall.*

p. 81, Newmyer, *John Marshall.*

p. 84, Albert J. Beveridge. *The Life of John Marshall,* 4 vols. New York: Houghton Mifflin, 1919.

p. 85, Newmyer. *John Marshall.*

Chapter 5

p. 87, Jean Edward Smith. *John Marshall: Definer of a Nation.* New York: Holt, 1996.

p. 94, Leonard Baker. *John Marshall: A Life in Law.* New York: Macmillan, 1974.

p. 101–102, Kermit L. Hall, ed. *The Oxford Companion to the Supreme Court of the United States.* New York: Oxford University Press, 1992.

FURTHER INFORMATION

BOOKS

Bjornlund, Lydia. *The Constitution and Founding of America*. San Diego, CA: Lucent, 2000.

Devillers, Dave. Marbury *v*. Madison: *Powers of the Supreme Court*. Berkeley Heights, NJ: Enslow, 1998.

Dwyer, Frank. *John Adams*. New York: Chelsea, 1989.

Lively, Donald E. *Landmark Supreme Court Cases*. Westport, CT: Greenwood, 1999.

Morris, Jeffrey. *The Jefferson Way*. Minneapolis, MN: Lerner, 1994.

Patrick, John J. *Supreme Court of the United States: A Student Companion*. New York: Oxford University Press, 2000.

WEB SITES
American Bar Association
www.abanet.org
Provides articles on legal issues along with other information
about federal and state courts, judges, and lawyers

FindLaw
www.findlaw.com
Provides Supreme Court opinions as well as other federal
and appellate courts

History of the Federal Judiciary
http://air.fjc.gov/history/about_bdy.html
Gives information on the history of the federal courts, all
the judges who have served, and landmark legislation

Supreme Court Historical Society
www.supremecourthistory.org
Allows access to opinions on landmark Supreme Court
cases

The Supreme Court of the United States
www.supremecourtus.gov
This is the official site of the Supreme Court. It provides
information on the history, rules, structure of the court,
as well as opinions on all the cases ever argued

U.S. Courts
www.uscourts.gov
Provides the latest news about the judicial system and
gives information about the structure of the courts

ACCESS TO THE SUPREME COURT

One of the most exciting experiences one can have is to visit the Supreme Court of the United States while it is in session. The courtroom (at 1 First Street, N.E., Washington, DC, 20543) has seating for three hundred, and those seats are available on a first come, first served, basis. The Court is in session to hear arguments from 10 a.m. to noon and from 1 p.m. to 3 p.m. on Monday, Tuesday, and Wednesday, for two weeks each month, beginning on the first Monday in October and continuing until the end of April each year. Sometimes, a session is held on Monday of the third week of the month. From May through June, starting at 10 a.m., the Court delivers its opinions on cases they have heard earlier in the year.

If you aren't able to attend a Court session, you can still tour the building every week of the year from Monday through Friday from 9 a.m. till 4:30 p.m., except on holidays. More than 700,000 people visit the Supreme Court Building each year.

BIBLIOGRaPHY

Baker, Leonard. *John Marshall: A Life in Law.* New York: Macmillan, 1974.

Beveridge, Albert J. *The Life of John Marshall.* Four volumes. New York: Houghton Mifflin, 1919.

Hall, Kermit L., ed. *The Oxford Companion to the Supreme Court of the United States.* New York: Oxford University Press, 1992.

Loth, David. *Chief Justice Marshall and the Growth of the Republic.* New York: Greenwood, 1949.

Malone, Dumas. *Jefferson the President: First Term 1801–1805.* Boston: Little, Brown, 1970.

Mapp, Alf J. Jr. *Thomas Jefferson: Passionate Pilgrim.* New York: Madison, 1991.

Newmyer, R. Kent. *John Marshall and the Heroic Age of the Supreme Court*. Baton Rouge: Louisiana State University Press, 2001.

Smith, Jean Edward. *John Marshall: Definer of a Nation*. New York: Holt, 1996.

Stites, Francis N. *John Marshall: Defender of the Constitution*. Boston: Little, Brown, 1981.

Articles
"America Rediscovers the Founding Fathers," *Washington Post*, March 31, 2002.

Balkin, Jack M. "The Use That the Future Makes of the Past: John Marshall's Greatness and Its Lessons for Today's Supreme Court Justices," *William and Mary Law Review*, 43, 2002.

Clinton, Robert Lowry. "How the Supreme Court Became Supreme," *First Things*, January 1999.

Croddy, Marshall. "Controversial Dimensions of U.S. Supreme Court Cases," *Social Education*, 66, 2002.

Curtis, Charles Pelham. "A Strange Story about *Marbury* versus *Madison* in Salem, 1808." *Proceedings of the Massachusetts Historical Society*, October 1953– May 1957 71, 1959.

Garraty, John A. "The Case of the Missing Commissions." *American Heritage*, 14, no. 4, June 1963: pp. 7+.

"James Madison." *Encyclopedia of World Biography*. Detroit: Gale, 1998.

"John Marshall." *Historic World Leaders*. Detroit: Gale, 1994.

Melhorn, Donald F. Jr. "A Moot Court Exercise: Debating Judicial Review Prior to *Marbury* v. *Madison*," *Constitutional Commentary* 12, no. 3 (Winter 1995), pp. 327-354.

Orth, John V. "How Many Judges Does It Take to Make a Supreme Court?" *Constitutional Commentary*, 19, 2002.

Perry, Barbara A. "The Cult of the Robe: The U.S. Supreme Court in the American Mind," *Social Education*, 66, 2002.

Rosen, Gerald E., and Kyle W. Harding. "Reflections Upon Judicial Independence as We Approach the Bicentennial of *Marbury* v. *Madison*," *Fordham Urban Law Journal* 29, no. 13, February 2002: p. 791+.

"The Case That Made the Court," *Wilson Quarterly*, 27, Summer 2003.

"Two Supreme Court Justices for Their Times," *Washington Post*, February 10, 2002.

Wernick, Robert. "Chief Justice John Marshall Takes the Law in Hand." *Smithsonian* 1998, 29, no. 8: pp. 157+.

"William Marbury." *Biography Resource Center.* Detroit: Gale, 1999.

index

Page numbers in **boldface** are illustrations, tables, and charts

aBOUT THE auTHOrS

corinne J. naDen is a former U.S. Navy journalist and children's book editor. The author of more than eighty nonfiction books for young readers, she lives in Tarrytown, New York. *Marbury v. Madison: The Court's Foundation*, is her first book for Benchmark Books.

ROSe BLUe, a native of Brooklyn, New York, has published more than eighty fiction and nonfiction books for young readers. Two of them have been adapted and aired by NBC television network. *Marbury v. Madison: The Court's Foundation*, is her first book for Benchmark Books.